Developing Executive Functioning
in the Early Years

Developing Executive Functioning
in the Early Years

Dr Rosalyn Muir

amba press

Copyright © Rosalyn Muir 2024

All rights reserved. No part of this book may be reproduced or transmitted in any form or by any means, electronic or mechanical, including photocopying, recording or by any information storage and retrieval system, without prior permission in writing from the publisher.

Published by Amba Press
Melbourne, Australia
www.ambapress.com.au

Editor – Rica Dearman
Cover Designer – Tess McCabe

ISBN: 9781923215443 (pbk)
ISBN: 9781923215450 (ebk)

A catalogue record for this book is available from the National Library of Australia.

*To the unsung heroes in early childhood centres
who inspire and positively shape young minds every day*

Contents

Foreword	1
Introduction	5
Chapter 1: Why bother developing executive functions?	9
Chapter 2: Educators as gamechangers	21
Chapter 3: Self-regulation	37
Chapter 4: Organisation	51
Chapter 5: Working memory	61
Chapter 6: Attention	69
Chapter 7: Thinking flexibly	81
Chapter 8: Thinking about thinking	89
Chapter 9: SOWATT's next?	97
Chapter 10: Postscript to educators	105
Resources	107
References	131
Acknowledgements	135
About the author	137

Foreword

For many years one question has troubled me: If we know so much about the importance of executive functions and self-regulation – how they operate, what they enable, how they grow, and the behaviours and outcomes they contribute to now and into the future – why have we not yet found consistently effective ways to improve these abilities? I can think of few other aspects of early childhood development that have been ascribed so much promise – by one account, carrying the potential to "reduce a panoply of societal costs, save taxpayers money, and promote prosperity" (Moffitt et al., 2011, p.2693).

It has not been for a want of trying. Together, with Rosalyn, we reviewed the last 20 years of research that attempted to shift executive function and/or self-regulation in early childhood education and care settings – 85 studies in total, across 14 different approaches that ranged from mathematics to mindfulness to computerised brain training (Muir et al., 2023). Few showed robust effects on children's self-regulation and executive function growth, and fewer still showed gains that transmitted to untrained abilities.

My interest in this question is longstanding. Indeed, some of those studies we reviewed were intervention studies I had conducted. In one of them – the first large research grant I led – I was hopeful to have found a solution. We aimed to target *early* self-regulation and executive function, given evidence of their foundational importance and malleability in this period. We leveraged early childhood education and care settings to reach a broad cross-section of the preschool population, given near universal attendance from age three. Our theory of change considered in more complexity the underpinnings and mechanisms by which we could shift young children's self-regulation trajectories. That *Early Start to Self-Regulation* program (Howard et al., 2020) was successful in stimulating change in the participating educators' knowledge and practice, and significant improvements in children's executive function. Still, the outcomes were not of the size and scale that I had hoped. While one can never know for sure the assorted limiting factors that constrained program effects during its evaluation, my suspicion was that one limiting factor was not achieving our aim of a deep and authentic understanding of the 'what, why and how' of self-regulation development that was genuinely shared by the educators implementing the program.

Despite modest effects from that program, and my pivot 'back to the drawing board' to figure out what we are still missing, I retained hope for the approach. I understand that this position could be ill-advised, given comprehensive and flexible curricular programs show about the lowest rate of efficacy of any approach we reviewed. Still, this approach carries the ability to tap into a well-trained workforce that is similarly mobilised towards positive early child development and outcomes. It is a highly social and inherently self-regulation demanding context. It is well resourced. And, at least from the age of three, a vast majority of children attend one or more days per week.

The year after completion of the *Early Start to Self-Regulation* study, I received an email from an educator with 30 years' experience – and I say *experience* in every sense of the word. She had taught in Canada, England, Sri Lanka, Malaysia, Ireland, Peru, Spain and Australia, first as a primary school teacher, then various leadership and advisory roles and, at the time of our meeting, assistant head of teaching and learning at a school in Melbourne. She wanted to undertake a PhD under my supervision.

Specifically, Rosalyn had created and implemented a framework for developing executive functions and self-regulation in the preschool classrooms in the school where she worked. She wanted her PhD research to focus on this framework and program, subjecting it to the full might of scientific rigour and evaluation (or at least those that fit within the parameters of a PhD). After meeting to discuss her interests, ideas and plans, I agreed to join Rosalyn on that journey as her PhD supervisor.

Rosalyn's SOWATT approach had many similarities to my own, but our lens was different. Both programs were grounded in current best evidence, but Rosalyn's was less beholden and encumbered by intricacies like delineations between abilities (à la Miyake's tripartite model; Miyake et al., 2000). Instead, a core tenant of her approach was that to shift any of these abilities, you must address them all. With this I wholeheartedly agree. Although there may indeed be distinct dimensions of self-regulation and executive function, we do not tend to engage them in such isolated ways in everyday life. It follows, then, that our best chance to cultivate them is to practise them in ways that resemble how we will need to use them.

Across months of meetings we discussed, extracted and articulated what was implicit in Rosalyn's SOWATT theory of change. We pressure tested the program elements against theory and research, with Rosalyn making refinements where this was prudent. Finally, Rosalyn led an evaluation of the SOWATT program, analysing its impacts on educators' knowledge and practices, and children's executive function and self-regulation.

Where previous programs taking a comparable approach have tended to generate small or no effects, the preliminary evaluation of SOWATT proved an exception. Changes were found in educators' knowledge and practice. Children improved in each of the outcomes evaluated. While the initial evaluation was small, the program's effects were statistically large. In short, Rosalyn showed that the SOWATT program can yield tangible benefits for its participants.

This book brings to life the ingredients that comprise the SOWATT program. For educators, it transforms obscurities of the underpinning science into meaningful, compelling ideas and actions for educators.

Its play-based approach means that children experience the program through everyday interactions and play.

I retain a firm belief that parents and educators are our best hope for realising population-level growth in early self-regulation and the promise of broad cumulative benefits that arise therefrom. Programs like SOWATT may well be the vehicles that help us achieve this. So, for educators interested in learning more about how to support the development of self-regulation (and related abilities) in young children – and I know there are many, given self-regulation is often cited as early childhood educators' number one most pressing concern – I highly recommend reading on.

Professor Steven J Howard
Early Start & School of Education
University of Wollongong
Wollongong, NSW, Australia

Introduction

Ask any parent what they ultimately want for their child and the answer is likely to be, "Happy". The follow-up question, "What does that look like for you?" is rarely asked. This may be because, at a gut level, we all share that goal and there is little need to unpack it further. We want all children to thrive, to be the best they can be academically, physically and social-emotionally. All this is implicit in that single answer: "Happy".

In its report *Student Agency for 2030*, the Organisation for Economic Co-operation and Development (OECD) identified 'agency' as "an invaluable skill that students can use throughout their lives" (OECD, 2019). It recognises students as active agents in their learning, able to positively influence their own life and the world around them. Alongside this, is the expectation that students will know how to learn and exercise their agency across many contexts: moral, social, economic and creative. With a well-developed sense of agency, individuals will be able to achieve long-term goals and overcome adversity. Buried in the subtext is the statement that, "students need foundational cognitive, social and emotional skills so that they can apply agency to their own – and society's – benefit". However, exactly which cognitive skills are being referred to is unclear. My hunch is that they are executive functions.

Similar aspirations are evident closer to home. The Australian Early Years Learning Framework V2.0 (EYLF) clearly states that: "All young Australians become: confident and creative individuals; successful lifelong learners; and active and informed members of the community" (AGDE, 2022). Disagreement with these statements is unlikely, yet there is no mention of which specific skills underpin these aspirations, or how these skills are to be developed.

In education, we are constantly looking for a 'silver bullet' that will make learning easier, more engaging and our teaching more effective for all children. In our heart of hearts, we know that this just isn't possible, and yet, after more than 30 years in the profession, there is something that has taken my attention and is worthy of exploring further: executive functioning.

Traditionally, executive functions have been the domain of educational psychologists, as deficits in executive functioning are associated with learning difficulties such as attention deficit hyperactivity disorder (ADHD) and autism spectrum disorder (ASD). In my time as a teacher in Learning Support, I regularly read reports from psychologists with phrases such as: "Joshua has underdeveloped executive functions" or "Maya would benefit from developing her executive functions", yet no actionable advice as to how to develop them was provided. Thus, in frustration, I would ask the question, "So what?" On the rare occasions when strategies for their development were listed, it was obvious that *all* children would benefit from them, not just the ones with a formal diagnosis.

And so began my research into executive functioning and the development of the SOWATT framework. The more I researched, the more convinced I became that *all* the children in our classrooms would benefit from having an educator who not only understands what executive functions are, but more importantly, has a toolkit to intentionally develop them.

This book is the culmination of more than 30 years in education and my PhD studies. My aim is to introduce you to executive functions from both a theoretical and practical perspective. To demonstrate how these skills underpin the broad concepts of 'agency' and 'happiness', and the intended outcomes of developmental curriculums such as the EYLF V2.0. More importantly, I intend to bridge the gap from theory to practice – there is so much empirical evidence to support the intentional development of executive functions, yet they rarely feature on pre-service teaching courses, and very little professional learning is available for educators to upskill themselves once they enter the profession.

Examining your professional practice through the SOWATT lens will provide you with the ability to recognise the skills in action and reflect on how your practice may be tweaked to better develop these critical skills. An understanding of executive functions in action will provide you with not only a more targeted approach to their development, but give you the language and understanding to justify your practices to anyone who walks through your classroom door. My hope is that SOWATT will no longer be a question, but rather a potential answer to how we set children up to thrive.

A word about the layout of this book: it is my hope that you read the book from cover to cover, however, it is arranged so that you are able to dip back into it to quickly and easily access information on specific aspects of executive functioning. It is broken up into the following chapters:

- **Chapter 1** highlights the importance of focusing on executive functions in your classroom and provides an overview of their importance throughout the day.
- **Chapter 2** focuses on the importance of *you*, the educator.
- **Chapters 3–8** examine each of the elements of the SOWATT framework. To make them easier to find, look for the corresponding icon in the top-right corner of the page. Each of these six chapters follows the same structure and concludes with TIPs – Theory Into Practice strategies, i.e. how the theory can be applied in your daily practice. No doubt you will be doing many of the suggestions already, but bringing strategies to a conscious level will allow you to feel even more confident about your practice.
- **Chapter 9** focuses on some concrete steps to help you implement SOWATT.
- **Chapter 10** is about going 'all in', committing to making a start.

- The **resources section** offers a number of materials that will support you further as you start to intentionally embed executive function development into your practice.
- **References** have been included for you to do some further reading about this exciting and evolving topic.

Happy reading!

Chapter 1

Why bother developing executive functions?

"Experience without theory is blind, but theory without experience is mere intellectual play"

– Immanuel Kant

Did you know that:

- Executive functions permeate every aspect of our lives, from academic success to physical health and mental wellbeing.
- No one is born with them – only the capacity to develop them.
- Underdeveloped executive functioning is implicated in a range of clinical conditions that affect school performance, including – but not limited to – ASD and ADHD. The diagnosis of both these disorders is on the rise.
- Interventions targeting executive functions can help close the social inequities of birth.
- Executive functions are a better indicator of school readiness than early numeracy, early literacy skills or an IQ score.

- Achievement gaps during the schooling years can be largely traced back to differences in pre-academic and cognitive skills performance at school entry.

Executive functions are abilities we take for granted – except when they are not there!

They help us to navigate busy lives; organise our time to meet both work and social demands; mentally say 'no' to the temptation to buy something on offer when we don't really need it; plan holidays; and basically just get jobs done. Without them, life can become chaotic, certainly more challenging and frustrating. Students in school rely on these abilities to remember and follow rules; shift and maintain attention on the teacher or task at hand; get along with others; and control emotions. The lack of well-developed executive functioning skills makes learning new things more difficult. It can often be the reason that students don't thrive in school and start to disengage with the whole education system.

It could be argued that the development of executive functions has never been more important. Education reform has spurred a demand for students to take greater responsibility for their learning, and workplaces are evolving from stable to more dynamic models. Leaders are now seen as 'facilitators', and individuals are expected to manage their own careers. Social mobility, diversity, globalisation and technological advancements require people to process diverse types of information and adapt to a wide range of situations, often under tight deadlines, leaving little time for deliberation. In this increasingly unpredictable environment, we face the challenge of maintaining consistency and reliability in our behaviour, to be perceived as trustworthy, while also cultivating flexibility and innovation to stay relevant in our work, relationships and communities.

There is mounting evidence that indicates that children who enter primary school with underdeveloped executive function skills may struggle to catch up to their peers without the aid of intervention (Diamond, 2016; Harms & Garrett-Ruffin, 2023; McClelland et al., 2010; Raver & Blair, 2020). Diversity in children's early-life circumstances and experiences can further exacerbate inequities of access and opportunity (for example, a child who finds it difficult to sit still is less likely to complete tasks and is more likely to be viewed as a distraction for their peers). Unfortunately, this can often lead to the child having a comparatively poor relationship with their educator (de Wilde et al., 2016). Unchecked, this presents challenges to a child's ability to thrive, and increases the likelihood of disengagement from the education system. It is also associated with a consequent lack of employment opportunities, with negative implications for society as a whole (Moffitt et al., 2011).

The OECD clearly states that the way to achieve better school experiences is by investing in high-quality schooling, particularly in the early years. It claims that "those who struggle at early stages but receive adequate, timely support and guidance have higher probabilities of finishing [school], despite any difficulties in their family or social background" (OECD, 2012).

To demonstrate how important these skills are, take a look at some examples of executive functions in action in a preschool classroom.

Table 1: Children and how they might use their executive functions

Activity	Ways in which children might use their executive functions
Morning drop-off	- Saying "goodbye" to family members and not getting upset - Entering the classroom and organising their lunchbox/water bottle - Initiating a task
Morning meeting (large group)	- Listening to the educator talk about the plans for the day - Listening to the ideas and comments of peers - Raising a hand, taking turns and curbing the impulse to call out - Asking questions and sharing ideas that relate to the topic - Not getting distracted by other children or objects - Able to refocus their attention after a distraction

Activity	Ways in which children might use their executive functions
Indoor play (small group/individual)	• Playing in the 'home corner': role playing, listening to peers, sharing resources, using props creatively, regulating emotions when a peer dominates the group • Construction blocks: making plans about what to build, negotiating roles, listening to peers, regulating emotions when a peer accidently knocks down their creation • Jigsaws: manipulating pieces (mentally and physically) to find where they fit, monitoring progress by comparing progress with a picture on the box, paying attention to colour and shape of individual pieces, following through and persevering to complete the puzzle, packing all the pieces away at the end and returning it to the shelf • Storytime: listening and responding to questions, looking at details in illustrations, remembering the characters, remaining focused • Craft time: remembering and following instructions, planning, sharing resources, exploring different options, persisting until completion, emotional regulation when things don't go as planned
Music and movement (large group)	• Following instructions: singing, playing instruments or moving in response to the educator's cues
Transitions	• Packing up upon request • Switching attention from one activity to another • Emotional regulation, when not ready to pack up
Snack or lunchtime	• Helping to set up/clear up • Waiting until the appropriate time to eat and taking turns serving food • Engaging in conversations with educators and peers • Asking for help when needed
Outdoor play (small group/individual)	• Climbing the equipment: remembering the safety rules, waiting for a turn, regulating emotions when they find it challenging
End of the day	• Reflecting on what they enjoyed at Kinder • Putting personal belongings back in their backpacks • Separating from their friends

The message is clear: the sooner that executive functions are developed, the better. It therefore makes sense to adopt a proactive approach to their development in the early years rather than try and 'fix' deficits later on. The younger the child, the less effort is required to effect change. See the conceptual graph below (Figure 1).

On the flipside, this also means that children are more vulnerable to negative experiences at this time, so it is important to give them the best possible start in life and build strong foundations for future flourishing.

Figure 1: Conceptual graph of the brain's ability to change and the amount of effort such change requires

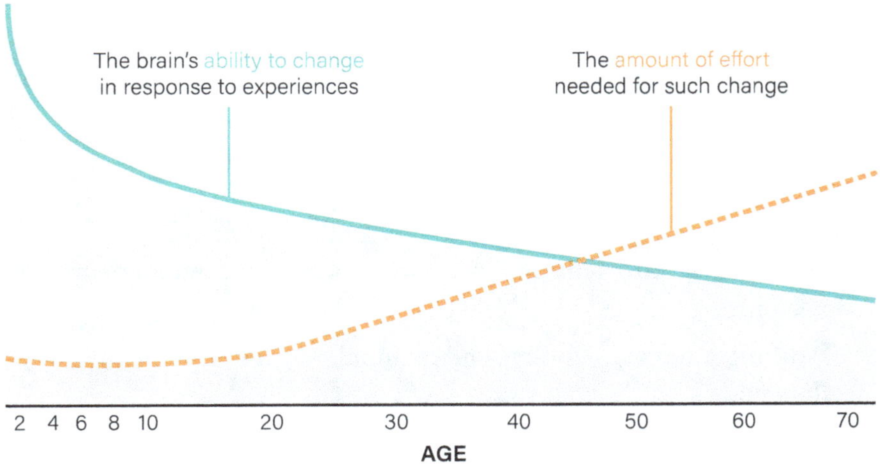

The brain's ability to change in response to experiences

The amount of effort needed for such change

AGE

Reproduced with permission from the Center on the Developing Child at Harvard University (developingchild.harvard.edu)

What are executive functions?

Defining exactly what executive functions are is tricky. Even researchers who have dedicated years of their life to their study are still unable to agree on exactly which skills make up this umbrella term. I, therefore, make no apology for simplifying the research. My aim is to make it accessible to the people who need it most and who need to understand it at the operational level in the classroom. The reason definitions are difficult is because the research has been conducted across a number of fields, including developmental cognitive neuroscience and developmental psychology. Moreover, most mainstream educators are blissfully unaware of executive functions, since pre-service courses rarely mention them. Educators who have taken special education courses may be luckier. However, this highlights the typically deficit approach that has been adopted to their development in the past. Executive functions are important for *all* children.

A formal definition of executive functioning is that it is a multidimensional construct that encompasses a set of higher-order, top-down cognitive processes, which are elicited when flexible, coordinated, goal-directed behaviour is needed (Diamond, 2014). Put in very simple terms, they may be described as the 'cognitive toolkit of success'. They are typically manifested in behaviour and allow us to not only regulate our thoughts, emotions and actions, but also to manipulate thoughts and information. They are called upon when automatised routines are not sufficient, or not possible, for example, in novel situations.

Three skills are frequently highlighted as being the core executive functions:

1. **Inhibitory control** – the ability to stop or suppress predominant responses.
2. **Working memory** – holding and manipulating information in the mind.
3. **Cognitive or mental flexibility** – the ability to shift attention and to think in different ways.

However, many researchers, myself included, would argue that executive function is broader than this, although no agreement has yet been reached about exactly which skills fall under the executive function umbrella.

In the SOWATT framework, an additional three executive functions have been included. The reason for this is because in the classroom we want to develop more than the core abilities, particularly if educators take a holistic approach to their practice, as is consistent with typical developmental curriculums. Intentionally embedding practices and experiences throughout the day that 'foster' holistically, rather than 'train' specific aspects of executive function and self-regulation, would, therefore, benefit from the additional focus on organisation, attention and metacognition, aka thinking about thinking.

The SOWATT framework is made up of:

Self-regulation
Organisation
Working memory
Attention
Thinking flexibly
Thinking about thinking

What is important to note, however, is that although these executive functions are generally accepted as being distinct abilities, they are also interrelated. For instance, in order to use inhibitory control skills, a child needs working memory to keep the appropriate alternative (rather than the impulsive response) answer in mind. To remember this alternative response, the child needed to have been focusing attention to the information in the first place. Therefore, in the preschool years, many researchers have found that executive functions appear more as a 'unitary construct', meaning they are so interrelated, it is difficult to isolate individual executive functions. This highlights one of the problems researchers encounter when they try to measure a young child's executive function. It is virtually impossible to isolate an individual executive function because assessment tasks will invariably draw upon more than one executive function simultaneously. When adopting a holistic approach to their development in the early years classroom, however, there is less pressure to worry about measuring individual executive functions – this can be left to clinicians.

Scenarios have been presented for each of the individual SOWATT elements, however, when reading them it soon becomes obvious that children are drawing on so much more than the highlighted skill. The purpose of these scenarios is to illustrate how you can make a specific executive function the targeted teaching point and hone in on its development.

The development of executive functions

Thanks to advances in technology over the past two decades, and the use of MRI and fMRI scanners, our knowledge of what is happening in the developing brain has improved significantly. We now know that executive functions emerge early in life, with periods of rapid development in the preschool years and again in early adolescence. In the preschool years, their development is associated with overall brain growth, while brain changes in adolescence are influenced by increased myelination* and synaptic pruning*.

Scientists generally agree that the prefrontal cortex (PFC) – the area shaded yellow in Figure 2 (opposite) – is the area of the brain with the greatest influence on the development of executive function skills. The PFC is highly connected with, and coordinates activity in, many areas throughout the brain. Because of this, it has been likened to an air traffic controller or the conductor of an orchestra. The interconnectivity of the PFC with brain areas associated with emotion and stress is particularly important from an educational perspective. When we are stressed, sad, lonely or not in good physical health, our PFC does not get to work properly, and thoughts can get easily hijacked by our amygdala – the almond shaped part of our brain that deals with emotion. Conversely, our ability to reason, exercise good self-control and flexibly adapt to change is much better when we are more relaxed, not stressed, feel emotionally and socially nourished, and are in good health.

The good news is that no one is born with executive functions in place, but we do have the capacity to develop them given the right conditions – these will be explored in detail in Chapter 2. Brains are built over time and the PFC is the last part of the brain to be fully developed – it usually reaches full maturity at around 25 years of age, and can be slightly later in males.

---

* myelination – the formation of the myelin sheath around a neuron to allow for improved conduction of messages
* neurons – brain cells that send and receive electrical and chemical signals
* synaptic pruning – the process where the brain eliminates extra neurons and synapses, which can help increase the efficiency of the brain's neural transmissions

This protracted development makes it susceptible to environmental and experiential influences – both positive and negative.

It is also important to stress that these skills do not develop in isolation of each other, nor do they follow neat linear trajectories. Without getting into a debate about the complexities of executive function development, there is evidence to suggest that babies as young as six months exhibit inhibitory control in their ability to inhibit neonatal reflexes and reaching responses. With respect to memory, the speed and efficiency with which infants encode information rapidly increases in the first few months. However, the ability to hold information in the mind and manipulate it, which is referred to as working memory, is far slower to develop.

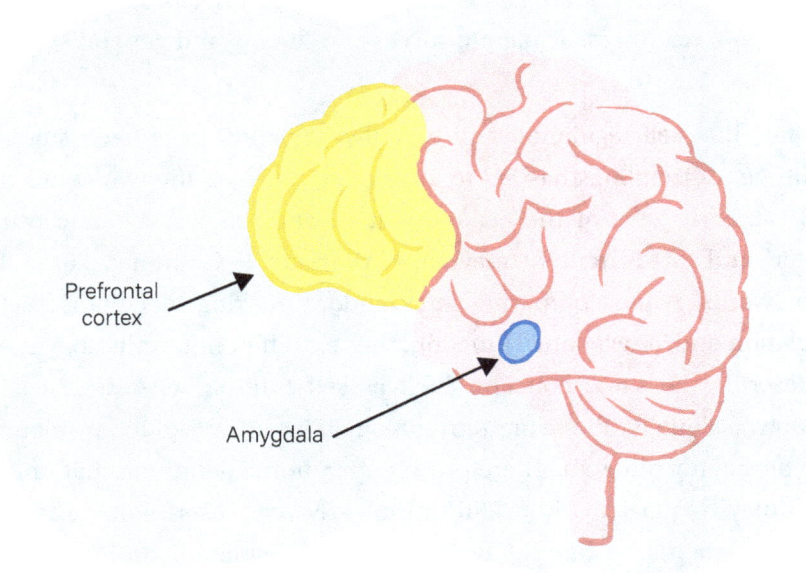

Figure 2: The prefrontal cortex

From an early childhood educator perspective, this is another piece of good news because the preschool years – typically between the ages of three and five – are a critical period for brain development for children. In fact, the brain is 90% developed by the age of five. Consequently, the early years are an optimal time to intentionally target strong brain architecture. If we can build strong neural pathways based on positive practices, we are on our way to setting children up for success.

What is the relationship between self-regulation and executive functions?

Most educators will be familiar with the term 'self-regulation'. Invariably, it is a term associated with behaviour – more often than not, dysregulated behaviour. This is not surprising given that Australia has been identified as having some of the worst classroom behaviour in the world (OECD, 2023), and good classroom management is seen as a priority. Self-regulation will be unpacked more fully in Chapter 3; however, it is important to know that executive functions have a lot in common with self-regulation. This is because they have both been identified as being critical skills associated with school readiness, academic success, wellbeing and general success in life.

The fact that self-regulation and executive function have been studied in different disciplines has led to an overlap between the two concepts. This is clearly seen at the academic level and has led to 'conceptual clutter' and 'measurement mayhem' (Morrison & Grammer, 2016). In other words, when comparing interventions seeking to enhance self-regulation and/or executive function, there is different terminology used to describe the same concept, such as self-control, self-restraint and willpower. Equally, the same terminology is used, yet its interpretation may be slightly different. Therefore, an operational definition that unites them may be particularly useful in the early years classrooms. Broadly speaking, then, the aim of developing self-regulation and executive functions simultaneously is to improve children's capacity to monitor and regulate their behaviour, emotions and cognition to adapt to their context and achieve their goals within that context.

Although there is a lack of agreement as to exactly how self-regulation and executive function are related, numerous studies have demonstrated a bidirectional relationship across their development (Howard et al., 2021). Many researchers, and I believe many educators, too, are of the opinion that skills do not develop in isolation, and growth in one area will help growth in another. In practice, this means that improving self-regulation might allow children to participate more productively in a wider range of executive function-promoting activities and sustain engagement for longer periods, which in turn improves overall executive functioning.

Young children (and many adults!) find it hard to regulate their behaviour; they find it difficult to take turns and they struggle with delaying gratification. Very often this is because emotions are involved. It is when we find ourselves in emotional situations that executive functions need to kick in. The effect of emotions on self-regulation and executive function should never be underestimated and will be discussed in more detail in Chapter 3. The important point to make here is that executive functions are only involved when self-regulation is conscious and deliberate, i.e. when we purposefully modify our behaviour in order to achieve a goal. In reality, this is easier said than done. It takes practice for this to occur – another reason to start early, before bad habits have become entrenched!

While recognising the link between self-regulation and executive function, it should be stated that executive functions have functions in their own right. Both constructs are critical for learning and wellbeing, however, executive functions can function on their own, i.e. outside of self-regulation. Since they are domain-general skills, they underpin all aspects of the curriculum as demonstrated in the resources section of this book (see 'Learning outcomes linked to SOWATT' on page 108), where explicit links have been mapped onto the EYLF V2.0. Empirical evidence is also suggesting relationships between specific executive functions and curriculum subjects such as working memory and mathematics.

Studies have also found that children who benefit the most from executive function interventions are the ones who need them the most (Gerholm et al., 2019; McClelland et al., 2019). The importance of getting things right from the beginning and setting children up for success, therefore, needs to be a priority of the early years educator. Regardless of a child's starting point, I would agree with Martin Seligman (2004) that we need to pivot from "the disease model" to one that is proactive, to improve "normal lives" and make them more productive and satisfying. With that aim in mind, a focus on intentionally developing executive functions in the early years would be a step in the right direction.

> **Four takeaways from this chapter:**
>
> ○ Executive functions and self-regulation skills are vital for everyone. We need them to navigate busy lives, and they are associated with improved academic achievement and general wellbeing.
>
> ○ Executive functions are malleable – they can change and be influenced by both positive and negative experiences.
>
> ○ Early intervention is optimal – identifying children's strengths and challenges early on sets them up for success. It is easier to address any identified deficits when children are young, rather than leaving it until they are older.
>
> ○ The development of executive functions is too important to be left to chance!

Chapter 2

Educators as gamechangers

"A good education can change anyone. A good teacher can change everything!"

– Dr Sudhir S Balerao

How can executive function development be enhanced?

There is plenty of evidence that self-regulation and executive functions can be taught, practised and improved. A range of interventions have shown promise for promoting children's self-regulation and executive functions. Part of my PhD research involved conducting a systematic review of all the self-regulation and/or executive function interventions studies that have taken place in preschool classrooms, with typically developing children, during a 20-year period from 2000 to 2020 (Muir et al., 2023). It was important for me to limit the studies to those conducted in the classroom, since that is where potential gains matter most – not in a laboratory!

An initial search produced 641 studies eligible for scrutiny. From these, only 85 met all the selection criteria and were included in the final analysis. Nevertheless, when combined, these 85 studies included more than 12,000 child participants. It was possible to identify 12 distinct intervention approaches, namely: i) mediated structured play; ii) semi-structured creative play; iii) mindfulness; iv) social-emotional learning programs; v) curricula specifically targeting executive function/self-regulation development; vi) multicomponent training; vii) music; viii) mathematics; ix) language training; x) integrated arts program; xi) task training (including digitalised); and xii) physical activity.

After a great deal of analysis, no one approach can be singled out at this stage as being consistently better than anything else. There is definitely not a 'one size fits all'. Even when we find common factors across programs, we may not be able to pinpoint which of them matter most. The jury is still out on exactly which approach works best and for whom. There are a number of reasons for this, including the differences in the ways research studies are set up, for example, some researchers select one or two individual executive functions to study, whereas others target global executive function development. Some studies use outside experts to lead the intervention, while others train the classroom teacher. In other words, when it comes to comparing the effects across studies, part of the problem is the variety of parameters used in the design of the research. As mentioned in the previous chapter, the tasks used to assess executive functions are not 'pure', in the sense that a variety of skills are often drawn upon to complete them in addition to the executive function that is being evaluated, and this, too, makes it challenging to compare outcomes. It's a bit like comparing apples to oranges. Nevertheless, some promising insights did emerge from the more efficacious studies, and these have been incorporated into the content and design of the SOWATT approach.

Seven evidence-based principles underpin the SOWATT approach:

1. **Biology is not our destiny** – our genes might be the blueprint, but our environment and experiences affect *how* the brain develops (Jacob & Parkinson, 2015).

2. **Start early** – significant brain development in the preschool years provides an optimal time to intentionally enrich executive function development (Diamond & Ling, 2016).
3. **Repetition** – ongoing daily practice produces greater improvements than lessons only once or twice per week (Diamond & Lee, 2011).
4. **Challenge** – executive functions must be continually challenged at an appropriate level to see improvements – ideally at the ZPD (Diamond, 2016).
5. **Engagement** – executive function activities should be age appropriate, engaging and build self-confidence and agency (Raver et al., 2011).
6. **Transfer** – global training of executive functions = greater transfer effects (McClelland et al., 2018).
7. **Teacher knowledge** – this is more important than expensive equipment (Konovalov & Krajbich, 2018).

Based on personal experience, I would add an eighth one to this list: *Intentionality*. Educators may accept all seven of the above principles, but unless they intentionally make the effort to plan for, implement and conduct ongoing monitoring and evaluation, it is unlikely that executive functions will be enhanced to their full potential. Rather, their development will be left to chance.

The SOWATT framework

Figure 3 overleaf presents an overview of the SOWATT framework, which will now be unpacked from a positive perspective – in order words, focusing on the conditions that are optimal for executive function development.

On the left-hand side, you can see the factors that influence self-regulation and executive function development, namely genes, the child's environment, the child's experiences and the educator.

Figure 3: An overview of the SOWATT framework

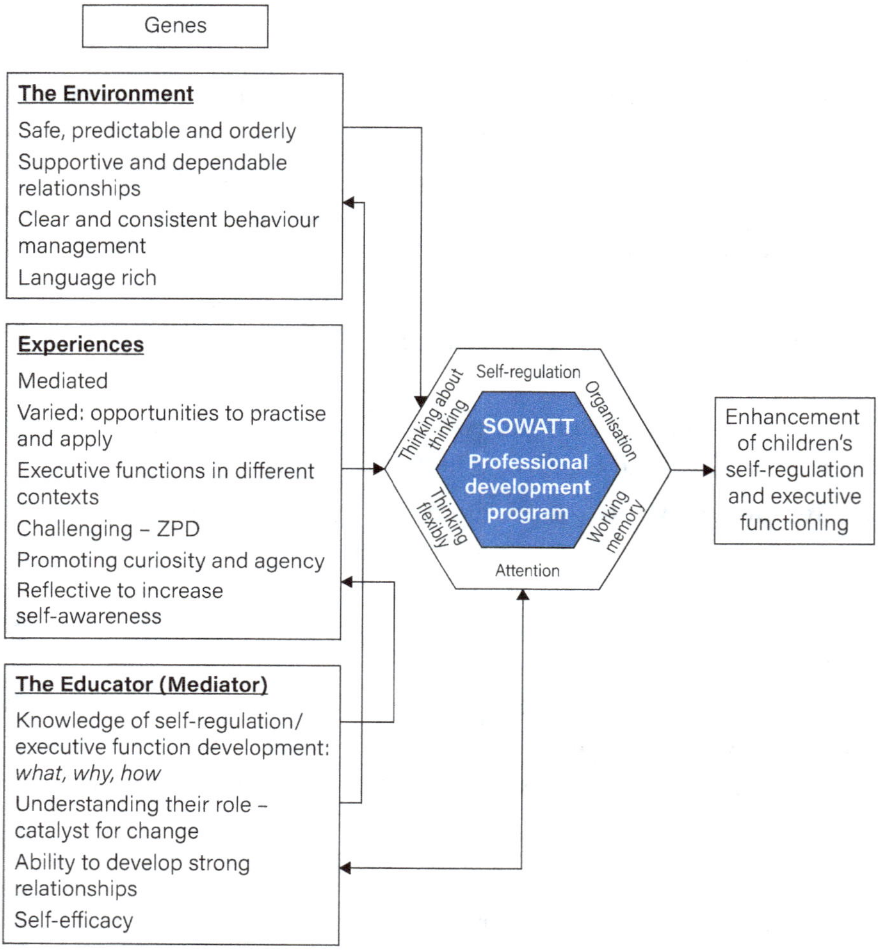

```
                    Genes
```

The Environment
Safe, predictable and orderly
Supportive and dependable relationships
Clear and consistent behaviour management
Language rich

Experiences
Mediated
Varied: opportunities to practise and apply
Executive functions in different contexts
Challenging – ZPD
Promoting curiosity and agency
Reflective to increase self-awareness

The Educator (Mediator)
Knowledge of self-regulation/ executive function development: *what, why, how*
Understanding their role – catalyst for change
Ability to develop strong relationships
Self-efficacy

SOWATT Professional development program

Self-regulation, Thinking about thinking, Thinking flexibly, Attention, Working memory, Organisation

Enhancement of children's self-regulation and executive functioning

Genes

Although there is little educators can do about a child's genes, it is worth remembering that genes may provide the blueprint for brain development, but this can be affected by the environment in which a child grows up and the experiences they have. Equipped with the appropriate knowledge, understanding and skills, educators are well positioned to control these two factors on an ongoing basis.

The Environment

Environment refers to both the physical and emotional environment of the classroom; we need to consider not just what it looks like, but also how it feels. In the preschool classroom, there are a number of elements that will help to support strong executive function development. A checklist of these to help you to conduct a personal audit of your classroom can be found in the resources section of this book (see 'The classroom environment through the SOWATT lens' on page 121).

Safe and predictable classroom environments may seem obvious; however, it is important to explain why this is vital. Depending on where you work, you are likely to have children from a range of different backgrounds in your class. Or, at the very least, from families with different approaches to parenting. The preschool classroom needs to be a place where children feel safe and have a sense of belonging, in order to thrive, regardless of their family circumstances. This is achieved in two significant ways: i) routines; and ii) good classroom management.

Routines help children feel safe, as by their very nature, routines are predictable. They are as crucial for the child who has separation anxiety leaving parents or caregivers in the morning as for the child who breezes into the classroom full of energy and raring to go. The former will be comforted with knowing there is a rhythm to the day, and the latter needs routines to keep their energy in check – two different causes of emotional regulation which clear morning routines can help to address. Our brains like predictability, they naturally look for patterns (Brackett). Doing certain things in a particular order at roughly the same time every day helps strengthen brain connections and builds children's self-confidence because they know what to expect. Children also learn to be more self-sufficient when routines are the same every day, since they are able to anticipate what comes next.

Good classroom management is proactive. It involves clarifying rules and expectations. Rules often have a negative connotation, but they don't need to. Even young children are aware of rules such as, not running across busy roads without looking or not touching a naked flame. Rules are fundamentally designed for our personal safety and the safety of others who are part of the communities in which we live. Presented in this way, rules support children's metacognitive development – there is a reason why we have them, when we take the time to think about them. If possible, involve the children in their creation – just remember to phrase them positively and don't have too many. Once you have agreed on three or four, be consistent in implementing them. Like routines, this can lead to reduced anxiety and provides external help for children to organise their behaviour, which is the ideal context for internalising regulation strategies.

Supportive and dependable relationships are also fundamental to strong executive function development. Many children in our classrooms do not come from homes where this is the situation. Your classroom may be the only place in a young child's life where they can find this. Get to know the children as individuals; get to know their 'currency' – in other words, know what makes them tick: their family, their interests, their favourite colour, the name of their favourite cuddly toy or footy team. When children are dysregulated, you can then draw on this information to distract/engage/persuade/comfort them and de-escalate emotional outbursts. Building strong relationships with each child is paramount for building emotional support, leading to reduced anxiety, increased engagement and curiosity, and more openness to challenges and even greater persistence.

It should be evident by now that the classroom environment needs to be a relatively stress-free environment. Stress is the enemy of thinking. The reason we can't think straight when we get stressed can be attributed to our amygdala (see Figure 2), the part of our brain designed to keep us out of danger. It's where our flight or fight responses are generated. These responses are extremely effective in life-threatening situations, but not so great when it comes to learning. The amygdala prevents thoughts from being processed in the PFC – the area of the brain associated with executive functions. If we want to unlock this gate and get our executive functions working, we need to convince it that we are not in danger. This is the same process in children as it is in adults. It is worth bearing in mind, therefore, that we need to get our own emotions under control before we try to co-regulate others.

A growing body of evidence highlights the importance of language-rich environments for young children. Language scaffolds thinking, therefore, if a child's oral language is underdeveloped, they are unlikely to be able to express their feelings and emotions verbally. Instead, they are more likely to resort to non-verbal language, which in highly charged emotional situations invariably includes behaviours such as hitting, kicking and screaming. The core features of emotional development include the ability to identify and understand one's own feelings. There is a need, therefore, to teach the language to describe emotions so that children can express themselves in words rather than physical actions. As Professor Marc Brackett says, "You need to be able to name it to tame it" (Brackett).

Language, and vocabulary development in particular, has been shown to be related to a child's family background. Children from lower socioeconomic backgrounds tend to enter primary school knowing fewer words than their higher socioeconomic peers. This gap usually remains throughout primary education, since vocabulary supports the early stages of reading development and is crucial for reading comprehension (Lervåg et al., 2018). It cannot be assumed, therefore, that children have the words to describe how they are feeling. No wonder their actions are often louder than words.

In the SOWATT approach, language may be viewed as 'the conceptual glue' that brings all the different parts together. Language facilitates executive functions to be practised in different situations and contexts throughout the day rather than at isolated times. In a typical preschool day, children interact with educators and peers across a variety of contexts (see Table 1 on page 11), such as educator-directed activities, child-directed activities and mealtimes. These contexts afford differing, yet equally important opportunities for instruction, interaction and engagement in and with executive function. Recognising language as one of the important mechanisms for change further highlights the recognition that learning, particularly in young children, is a socially embedded and active process.

It is for this reason that examples of the type of educator language that may be used to scaffold children's thinking and specific executive function development will be provided in the subsequent chapters related to the individual elements of SOWATT.

Essentially, the sample language phrases are based on the premise of extending children's conversations. This form of interaction, typically between an adult and one or more children, involves a sustained period of joint activity and thinking about a task or play. Essential is ongoing 'serve and return' dialogue, during which the adult's contributions serve to extend and/or protract the child's thinking. Used in this way, language also puts a focus on the process of learning, rather than solely the end product, encouraging deeper thought and reflection before, during and after activities.

Experiences

Much was made earlier of reducing stress in the classroom. This is not to be confused with challenge – indeed, without continually challenging our executive functions, they are not likely to develop.

This is significant when we start examining the experiences that are presented to children. Many readers will be familiar with Vygotsky's Zone of Proximal Development (ZPD), aka 'the sweet spot', aka 'the Goldilocks effect'. All these phrases mean the same thing – it is when learning is pitched at the perfect level: not too easy to become boring, and not too challenging to become overwhelming and frustrating. Unfortunately, both outcomes can lead to disengagement from the activity and increase the potential for dysregulated behaviour. Seymour Papert coined the phrase 'hard fun' to describe learning that sits on the edge of the ZPD. If a child is interested in and excited about what they are doing, they will usually invest the necessary effort into its completion. Hitting the sweet spot can be a question of trial and error, but like Goldilocks discovered, it's a wonderful feeling when it's 'just right'!

Planning for cognitive challenge is important and needs to be considered before starting an activity. It is not enough to simply provide an experience to practise a skill. If enhancing executive function is the goal, there needs to be incremental increases in difficulty, either in the level of cognition or complexity of the task. To clarify this, let's use the activity of Find the Pair – a familiar memory game played with a partner or small group. One way to increase the complexity of the activity is to add additional tiles. Conversely, reducing the number of tiles the children are working with lowers the complexity, making it easier for children to remember where the matching pairs are located. To make the same activity more cognitively challenging might involve a timer, requiring children to complete their turn within a limited time frame.

Finding the ZPD requires close observation and monitoring. It's about knowing your students and their capabilities, and knowing when to challenge and when to consolidate their learning. It is also about being open to the possibility that you are wrong – we have all had those experiences when children surprise you, being more able than you first thought. In addition to improved learning outcomes, strategically building cognitive challenge into our teaching actually increases student motivation and engagement. This, in turn, increases buy-in and perseverance to complete tasks. The bottom line is that children need to practise skills to get better at them, and they are not going to readily engage with activities that don't spark their interest and curiosity and, of course, provide them with some level of success.

As demonstrated in the first dot point below, it is possible to embed executive function language and expectations into transitions, morning tea and lunchtime. Again, this might require a bit of a shift to focus more on the process of learning, rather than the end product – a theme that will be highlighted further when exploring the elements of the SOWATT framework. When you make the brain work harder to complete more challenging tasks, it requires children to make connections with prior learning. This helps new knowledge to be remembered more easily, especially when it is linked to something that is of interest. In contrast, if a task is too easy, it gets completed without the need to draw on cognition or previous knowledge and is consequently often forgotten as soon as the task has ended.

Some more examples of how you might challenge children's level of cognition are:

- Increasing the amount of information given in instructions, for example, "First, I want you to pack up the blocks, then wash your hands ready for lunch and go and collect your lunchbox."
- Playing Pictorial Musical Freeze (see The Freeze Game on page 128) – starting with poses that require individuals to work by themselves, then working with a partner to do the same, then finally using a pose that requires a small group.
- Playing Red Light, Purple Light (see page 128) and gradually introducing more rule changes and coloured cards.
- Playing "I went to market ..." style games with numbers as well as items, for example, "I went to market and I bought one banana, two chickens, three sticks of celery ..." To make it even harder for those children who are ready, consider using ordinal numbers and alphabetical ordering.
- In mindfulness activities (see page 48), gradually increasing the amount of time for children to sustain their focus.
- Providing opportunities for children to experiment with open-ended experiences rather than those with a set outcome or procedure. The teacher differentiates during the process, for example, exploring printing using various objects rather than simply printing a flower using a pre-cut block.

These examples clearly demonstrate that executive functions do not need a prescriptive curriculum to be developed. They are age-appropriate activities and can be embedded in the preschool classroom. Play-based learning is rightly a highly valued medium for learning – this does not need to change. The only thing that changes is the level of intentionality of the educator. If you are serious about developing executive functions, then executive functions need to be planned for and scaffolded *prior* to the experience, *during* the activity and even *after* the activity through reflective conversations. This requires educators to be mediators, i.e. able to pop in and out of children's activities (even free play) to raise or lower the level of cognitive challenge as appropriate.

It is NOT about controlling or leading activities; self-regulation will never develop in contexts where educators don't allow children some freedom to explore boundaries, have a degree of choice, offer their opinions and reflect on their actions (check out 'Listening and asking questions' on page 127 in the resources section). Overregulation on the educator's part leads to compliance, or obedience, not self-regulation. The real test is what happens when an educator isn't with the child – how does the child behave when the educator's back is turned if they have not been given the opportunity to be co-regulated? The child is then limited to their previous knowledge, experience or understanding that is stored in their memory and will respond accordingly.

Therefore, experiences that encourage children's agency should also be promoted. Agency refers to the ability to "make choices and decisions to influence events and to have an impact on one's world" (AGDE, 2022). Supporting children's agency is about recognising that they have a right to make choices and decisions, and are capable of initiating their own learning.

It is also about recognising that agency requires well-developed executive functions. After all, making informed choices and decisions involves rationally and calmly (*self-regulation*) weighing up options (*thinking flexibly*) in order to arrive at a satisfactory outcome. It involves, goal setting and planning (*organisation*) and not losing sight (*working memory*) of these goals or getting distracted (*attention*) along the way. Once again, language plays a vital role in achieving this.

Ask questions that give children the opportunity to initiate and lead their own learning:

- What do you think?
- What do you want?
- Why?
- How can we do this differently? (Or safely, enjoyably, easily …)

Consider doing the following:

- Promote independent exploration and appropriate risk-taking.
- Promote independence and self-help skills through the opportunity to participate in routine tasks like wiping the table after eating, setting up environments and selecting resources.
- Promote learning through play-based activities that children plan and are relevant to their interests and other learning.
- Facilitate self-help skills as opposed to doing tasks for them.
- Ensure children's ideas and interests are included in plans such as outings and learning activities.
- Help children learn from their mistakes. Although it may be quicker, and/or make you appear kinder, to clear the path of obstacles for our children, 'failing safely' and learning from mistakes is an important skill for them to develop, especially when followed by process-orientated conversations that lead to new opportunities.
- Involve children in goal-setting activities. Help them define their goals and then support them in achieving them.

Please note, we are not trying to develop self-centred, opinionated individuals. When we place 'independence' within the wider context of community, we help children to recognise the value of thinking about themselves as well as others. They can then begin to understand the responsibilities that go with being an individual and a member of wider society – perhaps this was one of the lessons that the COVID lockdowns taught us!

The Educator

In the SOWATT approach, the final, and most important, factor impacting executive functioning is the educator. When empowered with the *why*, *what* and *how* of executive functioning, the educator can be the catalyst for change. As indicated by the arrows in Figure 3 (see page 24), it is the educator who has the capacity to impact their classroom environment and the experiences they offer on a daily basis. This encourages a focus on *fostering* executive functions, rather than *training* them, which allows them to be practised in different contexts throughout the day. It requires adopting a broader, more holistic approach to their development, which aligns perfectly with most developmental curriculums. Indeed, the EYLF V2.0 explicitly states that, "children's learning is dynamic, complex and holistic ... with all aspects intricately interwoven and related" (AGDE, 2022, p.8). It also requires that educators are involved in the change process because it takes time to embed practices throughout the day – an approach not conducive to the external expert who wants to pop into the classroom for a short period of time to enhance skills through the delivery of a training program.

Your role, as an educator, should be that of a mediator. In other words, it is the subtle social interactions between the educator and the child that enrich a child's learning experience. Learning about executive functioning and its role in self-regulation empowers you to make informed choices and apply an executive function lens on tasks that have probably never been considered previously. Take, for example, the activity 'Threading' – this is typically viewed as an activity to promote fine motor skills. Nevertheless, viewed through the SOWATT lens, and adding the challenge of copying, extending or creating patterns, it also provides an opportunity for potential behavioural and cognitive challenge, for example: planning, monitoring, adjusting and reflection.

Given that over 88% of children (in Australia) attend preschool centres in the year before they attend formal schooling (National Scientific Council on the Developing Child, 2010), an educator's impact can be both sustainable and far reaching. You are well placed to make lasting changes.

Context

Skills do not develop in a vacuum and each classroom context will be unique. We do not know exactly and to what degree culture affects executive function development. We do know, however, that values, norms, knowledge and preferences are subtly transmitted in the different contexts we move in. Research is telling us that differences exist between cultures, for example, culturally specific habits support delaying gratification in some countries, such as waiting to eat in Japan, that are not so prevalent in others (Doebel, 2020). In the same vein, it has been noted that Chinese children may be better equipped with knowledge and values that support compliance with an adult's requests (Doebel, 2020).

It is important, therefore, to recognise that each time we interact with children, our broader system of norms and values (our culture) are embedded in these interactions. Be aware of the potential for unconscious bias coming into play. As educators, we need, therefore, to approach these situations with an open mind, not jump to conclusions and be aware of our own beliefs, values and attitudes, which we are subtly transmitting. It is also worth remembering that children and educators are human. There is a lot going on in everyone's lives and there will be days when even the most regulated person will not present their best self!

In Chapters 3-8, the individual elements of the SOWATT framework are unpacked. However, before delving into each of the separate elements, the diagram overleaf provides a concise overview of what to expect. While the six elements of the SOWATT framework are described individually, the model assumes they are interrelated and work together to achieve outcomes, with typical preschool experiences requiring several to be working together.

Figure 4: The SOWATT framework

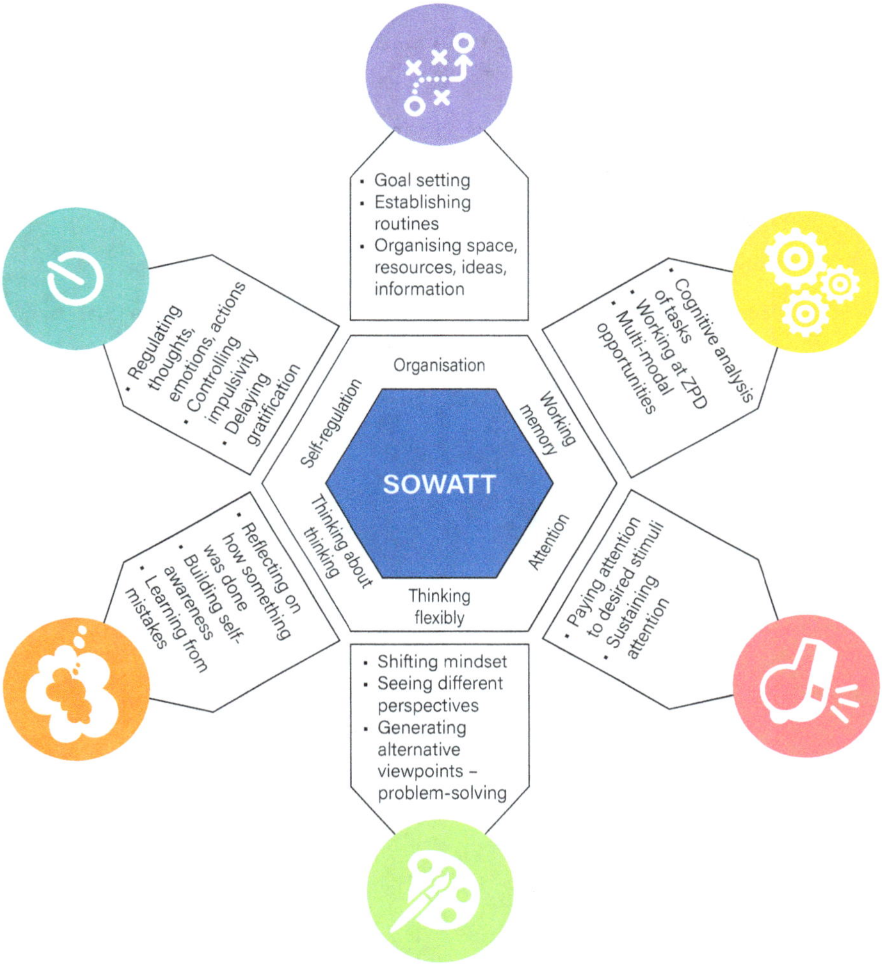

SOWATT

- **Organisation**
  - Goal setting
  - Establishing routines
  - Organising space, resources, ideas, information

- **Working memory**
  - Cognitive analysis of tasks
  - Working at ZPD
  - Multi-modal opportunities

- **Attention**
  - Paying attention to desired stimuli
  - Sustaining attention

- **Thinking flexibly**
  - Shifting mindset
  - Seeing different perspectives
  - Generating alternative viewpoints – problem-solving

- **Thinking about thinking**
  - Reflecting on how something was done
  - Building self-awareness
  - Learning from mistakes

- **Self-regulation**
  - Regulating thoughts, emotions, actions
  - Controlling impulsivity
  - Delaying gratification

Educators as gamechangers 35

Four takeaways from this chapter:

- The role of the educator is critical in the development of executive functioning.
- A focus on fostering, rather than training, executive functions is likely to lead to greater transfer of skills.
- A child's environment and their experiences impact executive function development.
- Language – both the child's and the educator's – is important in the development of executive functioning.

Chapter 3

Self-regulation

"I am, indeed, a king, because I know how to rule myself"

– Pietro Aretino

What is it?

Self-regulation is a multifaceted concept. One way to think about it is to consider it being made up of three main parts: behavioural, cognitive and social and emotional.

Figure 5: The components of self-regulation

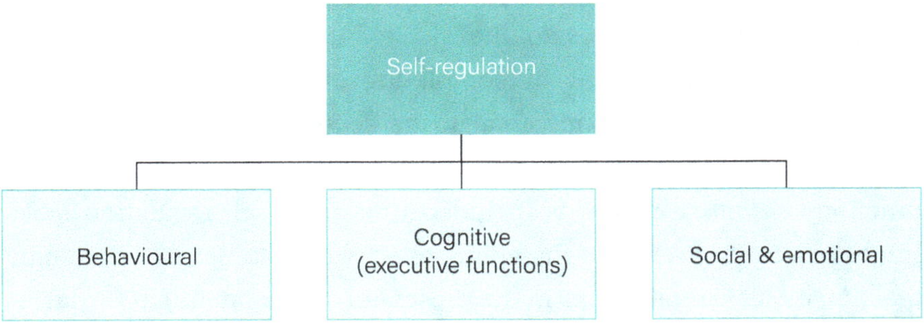

```
                    Self-regulation
                   /       |        \
          Behavioural   Cognitive    Social & emotional
                     (executive functions)
```

As the name suggests, *self*-regulation entails regulation by oneself (intrinsic), as opposed to being regulated by others. Although there are different aspects to it, they overlap and work together to create behaviour that is self-regulated.

Behavioural regulation

Behavioural regulation involves the ability to integrate working memory (for example, to remember and follow instructions), attention (for example, maintain focus on a task and ignore distractions) and inhibitory control (for example, override impulsive behaviour). When these processes are integrated, children are able to regulate their behaviour to match the expectations of specific contexts, such as the classroom or a family party. There is rapid growth in its development around three years of age, which is likely to slow down at around seven years old. So, in addition to being an important developmental period for behavioural regulation, preschool is also when many children begin to regularly spend time with their peers, which provides plenty of opportunity for practising their behavioural regulation.

It is widely acknowledged that children who are better at self-regulating their behaviour may experience more positive peer relationships, such as peer acceptance and sociability. On the other hand, children with limited behavioural regulation are more likely to experience negative relations, including victimisation and conflict (Bautista et al., 2024).

Cognitive regulation

Cognitive regulation refers to the skill of focusing and maintaining attention, being persistent in completing a task and the executive functions that allow an individual to be self-directed, self-monitored, self-aware and self-motivated. In the SOWATT framework, the executive function *inhibitory control* is included under the self-regulation label. Inhibitory control refers to the ability to control automatic or dominant reactions. An example of this in the preschool classroom might be during 'mat time', when a child blurts out an answer to a question rather than waiting to be asked or putting up their hand. It could be wanting to play on the yellow bike when someone else is using it and pushing them off rather than waiting for a turn. Turn taking can be a very difficult lesson for young children to learn, since they are gradually emerging from their completely egocentric phase. Taking turns and sharing are important skills to master, and play-based programs, typically found in preschool settings, provide the ideal context in which to develop them.

Delaying gratification is also part of self-regulation, and in a world geared for instant gratification, it is difficult – even for adults. We all know the difficulty in resisting the urge to check our phones in response to the 'ding' of a text message or get our chocolate fix when we are trying to cut down on our sugar intake. Like inhibitory control, one major factor hindering its mastery is that it is closely linked to our emotions. The more emotionally charged the situation, the more difficult it is to suppress the desire for instant gratification.

Emotional regulation

Emotions have a profound impact on self-regulation. Some researchers talk about 'hot' and 'cool' executive functioning. 'Cool' aspects are drawn upon when we are engaged in tasks that do not tap into our emotions – usually abstract tasks such as sorting items based on colour or shape. On the other hand, 'hot' aspects of regulation tap into our emotions and motivation, for example, at times when we are frustrated or are expected to delay gratification for something we really want. Please note that tasks don't necessarily fall neatly into one category or the other, and it might be as simple as an accidental knock of the arm causing paint to be splashed on the wrong part of a picture to turn a calm painting activity from a 'cool' to a 'hot' situation.

You may be familiar with the expression 'fight or flight', which is a physiological reaction to a perceived threat. In young children, this response can be particularly pronounced due to their developing brains and limited self-regulation skills. Since young children have underdeveloped prefrontal cortices, they rely more heavily on the amygdala (the part of the brain responsible for emotions), leading to stronger and less controlled fight or flight responses, which in turn, will likely mean they have trouble making good decisions. As children get older and their prefrontal cortex matures, they become better at regulating their responses to stress and can more effectively manage their emotions and behaviours in the face of perceived threats. In the meantime, they need to be taught strategies to manage their reactions more effectively.

Without a basic level of emotional regulation, other aspects of self-regulation cannot flourish. It is no wonder, therefore, that stronger emotional regulation skills in early childhood are also associated with a range of positive outcomes, including academic and social development (Blair et al., 2010).

In essence, self-regulation is the ability to integrate cognitive and emotional aspects into behaviour that allows us to reach our goals. It's the ability to stop, think, *then* act, and is a skill that needs to be practised early and often.

Why is it important?

Self-regulation is one of the most important predictors of school readiness, academic achievement and lifelong wellbeing. Rightly or wrongly, school systems are built around students' ability to self-regulate; from the prep child expected to sit still on the mat while the teacher gives instructions to the high school student who is expected to keep their focus solely on the document on the screen and resist the urge to check their social media sites in class.

In early childhood settings, children with poor self-regulation will often get themselves into trouble through impulsive behaviour. Studies have found an association between a child's poor self-regulation and a negative relationship with their educator (Trentacosta & Shaw, 2009). In the longer term, poor self-regulation in early childhood has been associated with an increased risk of developing later behaviour problems, greater risk-taking behaviour in adolescence and disordered behaviour as adults. Therefore, being able to self-regulate benefits not only young children, but society as a whole.

What is happening in the brain?

The limbic system, including the amygdala, processes emotions. When a child experiences strong emotions, the amygdala is highly active. The brain's reward system, involving the neurotransmitter dopamine, reinforces behaviours. When a child successfully self-regulates and receives positive feedback, or experiences a positive outcome, dopamine is released, reinforcing the behaviour and encouraging the child to repeat it in the future. Through repeated practice of self-regulation strategies, children strengthen the neural pathways, making it easier for them to access their prefrontal cortex, the part of the brain responsible for decision-making processes.

Behaviour

When a child is having difficulty with self-regulation, you are likely to see these sorts of behaviours:

- An inability to stop and think before acting
- Interrupting conversations
- Speaking out of turn
- Easily frustrated and quick to anger
- Difficulty keeping their cool when someone annoys them
- Difficulty sitting still
- Lacking perseverance
- Difficulty taking turns
- Difficulty sharing resources
- Getting overexcited when something special is happening
- Difficulty calming down when upset

- Difficulty controlling impulses
- Waiting/delaying gratification

Self-regulation in action

Picture a preschool classroom where a painting easel has been set up in one corner. Mia and Ella are either side, busily creating their masterpieces and chatting to each other at the same time. A few minutes into the experience, Ella decides she wants to see Mia's painting and with a paintbrush loaded in scarlet red paint, she darts around to the other side of the easel. As she does, she waves her brush and a big glob of red paint lands on Mia's paper.

"Noooo!" screams Mia, loud enough to get everyone's attention, including Ms Jade who makes her way to the painting area. In the short time it takes her to arrive, Mia is howling and Ella has retreated back to her side of the easel, trying to look busy.

Between Mia's sobs, Ms Jade pieces together what happened. She asks Ella to put down her brush and come and have a talk. After a short chat, which included an apology from Ella, the three of them think about how the unwanted red splodge can become part of the painting. Eventually, Mia settles for making it into a flower and peace is restored once more.

How is self-regulation enhanced?

The majority of children in the preschool classroom will struggle to self-regulate, after all, it is probably the first time that they find themselves in a context where they are not the centre of attention. There will be many others of the same age competing for the adults' limited time. Therefore, educators need to become *co-regulators*, which means using *intentional* interactions to foster the skill. Think of co-regulation like the training wheels on a bicycle. Co-regulation helps children practise self-regulation through adults' guiding behaviour. This allows for children to practise the skill safely, and build their self-confidence at the same time. It is considered essential for the progression from *other* to *self*. What this looks like in practice will probably be slightly different in different contexts, but there are some important strategies that can be used: modelling, scaffolding, mediating through language, providing feedback and definitely being proactive.

Modelling

Children are like sponges. They notice things, even things we don't want them to, like our habit of clearing our throat before we speak or sweeping the hair out of our eyes when it's in the way. As adults, we play a powerful role in influencing children's behaviour without even opening our mouths to give an instruction or engage in a conversation. We should, therefore, never underestimate the importance of modelling the behaviour we'd like to see in our children.

To a large extent, this is due to the work of mirror neurons: a set of neurons in the brain that fire not only when you perform an action, but also when you observe someone performing an action. Have you ever given any thought to when you yawn only seconds after seeing someone else do the same? This is an example of mirror neurons at work. Apparently, within 72 hours of being born, mirror neurons prompt infants to mimic the facial expressions they see. By six to eight weeks, babies have developed the combination of visual awareness and brain development to give a true "I know you" smile. These social smiles are the baby's response to the world around them. It is thought that mirror neurons may be responsible for why we can feel empathy or understand others' intentions and states of mind. Children are often better at picking up on adult emotions than we give them credit for. Take, for example, a child who has a hard time leaving their parent in the morning. All too often, it is the parent who has separation anxiety, not the child. They simply read the emotion and mimic it.

As educators, we need to think about our own behaviour. We can't expect children to display good self-regulation when they see an adult regularly modelling aggressive behaviour every time another car cuts in front of them on the way to school, or a parent getting irate when they haven't managed their time and are late for an appointment. In the absence of a mirror neuron 'off switch', be aware of the messages you are sending to children, and consider if this is how you want to be portrayed when children are engaged in creative play with their friends.

Scaffolding

This involves giving the appropriate level of support in order that children can complete a task. It is closely linked to Vygotsky's ZPD (explained in Chapter 2). It's about providing just the right amount of support to enable a child to be able to complete a task fairly independently. Based on the 'gradual release of responsibility' model, it supports children towards independence. Importantly, it recognises children as active, not passive, learners.

The key to learning self-regulation skills is not to avoid situations that are difficult for children to handle, but to coach children through them and provide a supportive framework, i.e. scaffold them. In practice, this involves setting up a positive, well-ordered classroom environment and planning experiences that provide opportunity to practise the skill in different contexts, including those likely to provoke greater emotional responses. Plan activities that require children to stop, think and then act.

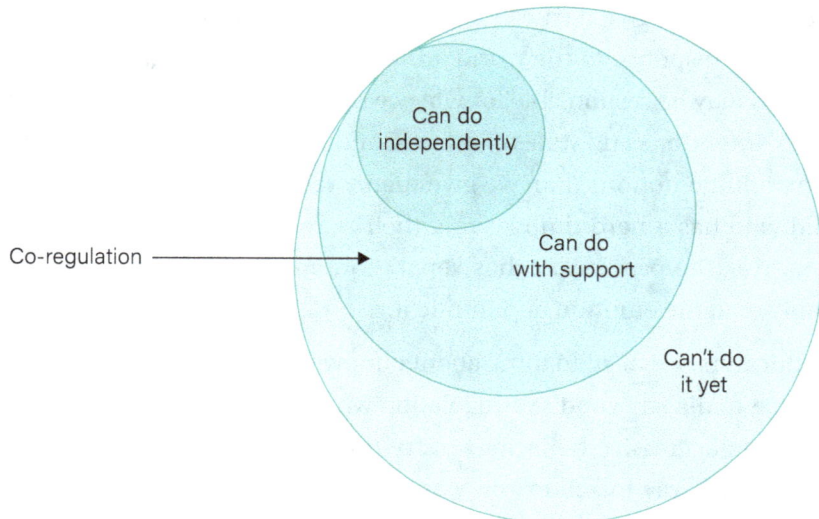

Figure 6: The Zone of Proximal Development

Language to support the development of self-regulation

Self-talk is a powerful tool in supporting children to self-regulate. When children engage in it, they can be seen repeating rules or instructions aloud. Repetition in this way helps children to internalise rules, making them more likely to regulate their behaviour according to societal norms and expectations. Self-talk also allows children to verbally walk themselves through the planning stage of an activity and is useful when they encounter a problem. As adults, we do this all the time, albeit in our heads. In order to model it, we need to share our thoughts out loud. For example, when you are reading a book, you might say, "I wonder what will happen next …" or, "No wonder Elmer felt upset, I wouldn't want that to happen to me either, that was very unkind of the other animals."

Table 2: Language that supports the development of self-regulation

Self-regulation
"Try to use your words, not your hands."
"I can see you're tired, let's have a little break and come back later."
"You have worked really hard, and you feel tired. Please can you try and finish this and then you can choose to do something else."
"Well done on keeping going, even though it's a bit tricky."
"Just a moment, let me think."
"I can see you're not very happy at the moment, why not have a drink of water and come back?"
"Well done on not getting mad, and for using your words to tell James what was bothering you."
"I like the way you are waiting patiently for your turn."
"I'm going to ask Malia as her hand was up and she was waiting patiently."
Teach the language, "Plan, Do, Review."
Practise affirmation statements: "I am calm" and "I am a good listener."

"It's your choice, either _____ or you can do _____."
"Take your time to think before answering."
"You need to calm down; let's get a drink of water."
"Stop, think, do."

Feedback

Studies have shown that providing feedback to children that is *timely* and *specific* (Hattie & Timperley, 2007) increases their self-awareness, which in turn, increases their self-regulation. With young children, this needs to be done when the action occurs. The exception to this is emotional meltdowns, which need to be addressed when the child is calm and not being hijacked by their amygdala. Any feedback given should be weighted in the positive, approximately four positive statements to one negative. Remember, the tone of the delivery is likely to be as important as the spoken word, and don't forget to make the feedback about the behaviour, not the child.

Be proactive/intentional

Anticipating where and when children are likely to be dysregulated and planning for this is a far better strategy than reacting to each situation as it arises.

Don't be afraid to explicitly teach children how they can be in charge of their thoughts, emotions and actions. Explain to them how hard it is to be in charge – even for adults! Share your behavioural expectations before tasks, so children understand how you are expecting them to behave. There is also growing evidence of the value of introducing mindfulness activities into the day. They don't have to take long and can easily be incorporated at times of transitions, for example, after outdoor play or before the start of the afternoon session. Teach children the joys of watching a toy move up and down as they practise belly breathing, or teach them simple 2D shapes through visualising them through their breathing patterns.

Be aware of transitions during the day; these need to be planned and calm. Have you noticed that emotions can be contagious? It can take just one child to disrupt the whole class. Try and limit the number of transitions as much as possible, have some clear routines and give clear instructions so that your expectations are clear before a transition begins. Assign one of the adults in the room to stay with the child who you know may struggle or have difficulty changing from one activity to another.

Consider having an area in the classroom that is quiet, where children can go if they need time out to calm down. It may be a carpeted area with books or audio stories, or even a cubbyhole which can provide a child with an extra sense of security if required.

An approach that has gained popularity over the past few years is **mindfulness**. One of the benefits of the approach is that it helps children learn what it feels like when they are calm. We often ask children to 'calm down', assuming they know what we mean. Unfortunately, this is not always the case, so we need to provide them with opportunities to help them experience this feeling. A range of resources is available on the market to support this practice, but in reality, it doesn't need to be overcomplicated. Teaching children to tune in to their breathing is an easy way to start; a minute of mindful breathing may be enough for children to 'check in' with themselves.

Menu of activities

Figure 7 overleaf provides some example activities that will help foster the development of self-regulation – it is an exhaustive list, but will help get you started. As mentioned previously, no task will draw exclusively on one executive function, but if these activities are regularly performed with a self-regulation lens, then at least you know you will have intentionally targeted its development.

A question to ask yourself is: "How can I make the activity easier/harder and hit the ZPD?"

Figure 7: Example activities to foster self-regulation

Self-regulation			
Imaginary play with peers	Musical Statues	Simon Says	Red Light, Purple Light
Meditation/ mindfulness	Pop bubbles with certain parts of the body only	Play games involving turn taking	Physical activities requiring a cognitive element
Yoga	Listen to interactive stories	Sing songs with specific actions	Guided meditation: Progressive Muscle Relaxation
Blowing bubbles	Teach box breathing	Make emotions in the mirror	Read stories that incorporate emotions of characters
"Settle your Glitter" Making glitter jars	Use a sand timer to calm down, i.e. 'time out'	Walk/stomp/ clap rhythms	Walk with a hand bell and try not to let it ring

Theory Into Practice strategies (TIPs):

- Model the behaviour you want to see, for example, you might ask if you can join in play, make adjustments so that others may join in play and demonstrate turn taking.
- Have clear, consistent expectations for behaviour, and give reminders.
- Build in movement breaks.
- Catch a child displaying desired behaviour and give positive feedback, i.e. draw attention to positive behaviour (not negative ones).
- Teach 'Stop, think, do' routinely and have a picture of traffic lights as a reminder.

- Use distraction in situations where emotions are rising.
- Teach strategies for what to do when waiting to gain an adult's attention, for example, "Excuse me, please," or hold a child's hand to show you've noticed them.
- Use humour to diffuse situations.
- Teach vocabulary associated with emotions – help children put feelings into words.
- Promote a child's sense of autonomy and responsibility – give them choices, as this is likely to increase their engagement in tasks and provide further opportunities to practise self-regulation.
- 'Redirect and re-engage' when you notice a child's heightened emotional state.
- Teach children the difference between 'have to' and 'want to'.
- Use a 'talking stick' that can be passed around the children as a reminder of who is speaking and the expectation to listen.

Chapter 4

Organisation

"Organising is what you do before you do something, so that when you do it, it is not all mixed up"

– AA Milne (*Winnie-the-Pooh*)

What is it?

Organisation refers to ordering, planning (sequencing and prioritising) and setting goals in relation to:

1. Physical space
2. Resources
3. Time
4. Information

Why is it important?

Successful organisation is needed in preparing for and completing most activities. The development of organisation becomes even more critical as the responsibilities and requirements of school and extracurricular activities increase each year. It is associated with better academic and non-academic outcomes for children (Konovalov & Krajbich, 2018). Goal setting and planning are important inclusions in this element, with a focus once again on intentionality by the educator and the child. Planning requires thinking about actions in advance and approaching tasks in a strategic, organised and effective manner.

What is happening in the brain?

The brain's ability to reorganise itself by forming new connections is called neuroplasticity. When children repeatedly practise organising, such as tidying up toys or planning their day, the neural pathways related to these tasks become stronger.

Behaviour

When a child is having difficulty with their organisational skills, you are likely to see these sorts of behaviours:

- Regularly losing their personal belongings
- An unawareness of classroom routines
- Attempting tasks in a haphazard way
- Difficulty initiating tasks
- Needing constant reminders or prompts about what comes next
- Not responding to time prompts
- Displaying a lack of ability to plan/sequence tasks

Organisation in action

While outdoors, children participate in a pretend play activity where they transform the playground into a camping adventure. Leah, the educator, provides various props and materials, such as tents, sleeping bags, flashlights and pretend campfire supplies. The children work together to set up the campsite, organise the equipment and assign

roles for different camping tasks, such as setting up the tents, gathering firewood and preparing pretend meals. To ensure the success of their camping adventure, the children must use their organisational skills to plan and execute each aspect of the pretend play scenario. They need to coordinate their actions, share responsibilities and maintain order within the campsite, demonstrating their ability to stay organised and work collaboratively.

After the activity, Leah sits with the children to reflect on all the things they needed to organise as part of the adventure, and through the conversation, children reach the realisation that making lists can be helpful in getting ourselves organised.

How are organisational skills enhanced?

Modelling, scaffolding and using targeted language are three important strategies to use to develop children's organisational skills.

Physical space

Classrooms need to be well organised, not only for everyone's safety, but also to promote children's growing independence. A well laid-out classroom allows children to move around easily. There should be no bottlenecks where children are likely to bump into each other. This increases the likelihood of children being upset and potential meltdowns as a result of a Magna-Tile tower being accidently knocked down by a classmate's elbow.

Be aware of the more popular activities that children seek out in your room and make sure sufficient space is available. Explicitly share your expectations regarding the number of children allowed at a tabletop activity and teach them what to do and say if they can't have a turn straight away.

Model good organisation. Keep a clean and tidy classroom – not to be confused with sterile and boring. Share some of the things you had to do today before the children arrived to ensure that the day ran as smoothly as possible. This shows the importance of the skill – and that it's not just for relevant for children!

Ask yourself these questions:

- Why have I set up our classroom in this way?
- What cues are there in this classroom that are going to help children remember our routines?
- How do the children know where the resources are kept?

Resources

Resources within a classroom are shared. Therefore, teach children the importance of putting them away when they have finished with them. No one really likes packing up after themselves, but it's all part of belonging to a community. The very act of sharing and thinking of others is one of the first steps towards developing empathy. Make this as easy as possible by having all small parts, craft and play equipment clearly labelled with the appropriate picture on the container and on the shelf where you would like it stored. It doesn't have to be a chore – make it fun by putting on a tidy-up song and singing together, or turning a sand timer over and getting the job done before the last grain of sand falls down. As Mary Poppins reminded us:

> *"In every job that must be done*
> *There is an element of fun*
> *You find the fun and snap!*
> *The job's a game"*

This not only builds good organisational habits, but also builds independence. After all, the more a child can do for themselves, the more time educators have to work productively with small groups or individuals.

Time

Time, in the sense of measured time, is a difficult concept for young children to grasp. There is a difference between the reality of time passing and how time feels. Much depends on the activity the child is engaged

in and the degree to which they are invested in it. Where possible, make time tangible by using sand timers of different sizes or use my personal favourite: a Time Timer, which silently counts down desired periods of time through the disappearance of the coloured disk, providing a simple 'ding' when the set time has expired. Time Timers can be particularly useful for the child you know who struggles with transitions and packing up, since they provide such a clear example of time passing.

One of the hardest parts about being an adult is juggling the many tasks that make up our day. As children get older and advance through their schooling, they are responsible for an ever-growing number of things both in school and outside. Prioritising could be considered the secret to being an effective time manager and, in spite of the abstract nature of time, children are generally quick to understand the idea of *sequencing* and *prioritising*. For example, they have little difficulty understanding that they need to put their socks on *before* they put on their shoes, and that they wash their hands *after* going to the toilet. Or "*First* you put on sunscreen, then your hat and *then* you can go out to play." So, using language that conveys a sense of time and order is an important step in developing children's organisational skills and, as part of this, supports their *planning* behaviour.

Information

There is a vast amount of information that is conveyed to children every single day. One example common to most classrooms is the daily schedule. Presenting this in a visual format not only models the concept of sequencing and planning, but also forms part of building classroom routines, which, as mentioned previously, plays a pivotal role in stress reduction.

When talking about the day ahead, consider asking children one thing that they want to achieve today (goal setting). I observed this in a classroom where the educator incorporated it into the daily 'Acknowledgement of Country'. The Aboriginal word *Wominjeka* means more than welcome; it means 'come with purpose'. As such, children were encouraged to state what their 'purpose' was for coming to Kinder, thereby introducing the concept of planning, and required them to engage their thinking, rather than simply reciting some familiar phrases.

Another way of scaffolding children's thinking around organising information is to make the planning visible, for example, record children's ideas as they are shared.

To illustrate this, picture Amy's class, which is planning to go on a bushwalk. Amy has a large piece of paper and a texta which she uses to record the children's suggestions of what they will need to take with them on the walk. As each suggestion is shared, she writes the child's name alongside it. (This works as a motivator for children to engage in the task, as they all want their name on that paper.) Having collected all the suggestions, Amy follows up with a series of questions that require children to organise the ideas according to things that she needs to prepare and things that each child needs to do. Two different-coloured circles around the suggestions soon makes this visible and this becomes their plan.

The value of getting children involved in planning processes in this way cannot be underestimated. The consequence of not doing so can lead to *learned helplessness* – something we want to avoid at all costs!

Menu of activities

Below is a menu that provides some examples of activities that can be used to foster organisation. Choose one or two to get you started and ask yourself: "How can I make the activity easier/harder and hit the ZPD?"

Figure 8: Example activities to foster organisation

Organisation			
Have a picture/photo of how you want the craft station to be left at the end of each session	Give children the opportunity to plan: an event, arts & craft, construction	Make deliberate mistakes to see if the children notice – holding the storybook upside down, counting incorrectly	Provide opportunities for unstructured time, empowering children to organise themselves
Have placemats with children's pictures for morning tea/lunchtime	Make up stories from sequenced pictures	Retell stories in the correct order	Plan the morning together (prioritise)
Cooking – or any activity that needs to be done in a particular sequence	Dramatic play	Draw a plan before building something	Set up experiences together: "What will you need?"
Have a class travelling bear or something that needs to be taken home and brought back to class on a rotated basis	Pattern-making activities, either threading beads or matching a predetermined pattern	Teach children how to do jigsaws by looking for the outside pieces first (only applicable to a rectangular puzzle)	Set up obstacle courses requiring a particular sequence
Ask children to recreate a Lego model from a picture	Tidying up/spring cleaning	Complete simple tasks within a time frame (use a sand timer)	Sort objects into different categories

Language to support the development of organisational skills

Table 3: Language that supports the development of organisational skills

Organisation
Use "When… then…" language.
Use words that signify sequence: first, second, third, next, after that, then, finally.
"What would happen if we changed the order?"
"Is order important here?"
"What equipment do you need in order to do this task?"
"Do we have all the equipment we need for this activity?"
"What do you think the problem is?"
"Where do you start?" "Where should we start?"
"What will you do next?"
"Compare this sequence to previous activities."
"We can tick off what we have done, so we know how much is left to do."
"There's a lot to do here, I think it would help to make a plan."
"Compare this pattern with the previous one; what do you notice?"
Celebrate it! "Great job getting all your things ready!"

TIPs:

- Use visual schedules and refer to them regularly.
- Establish consistent routines.
- Label all resources (pictorially) and make them accessible for children to access and put away.
- Model a tidy classroom.

- Use checklists and ask children to tick off things as they are completed.
- Model think alouds, "Hmm, where can I find the scissors?"
- Model planning behaviour and make lists of steps for a joint project.
- Provide time prompts prior to packing up – support with a song or visual timer.
- Make children who find tasks difficult the special monitor for a while, supervising the tidying up.
- Have a bank of printed nametags which children can independently access to label their finished paintings, making it easier to distribute them at the end of the day.
- Use temporal language: first, then, after, finally, the days of the week.
- Set goals together.
- Have visuals to track time: sand timers, Time Timer, countdown app.
- Provide opportunities for children to practise their organisational skills by providing choices.
- Support opportunities for children to plan an event, arts and crafts, dramatic play.
- Look around at things that are organised and talk about how they are organised, for example, the library, a car park, the dishwasher.
- Talk about things that *have* to be organised and why; pose the question: "Is there anything that doesn't need to be organised?"

Chapter 5

Working memory

"A central issue with working memory is that it's limited. It's limited in capacity, limited in duration, limited in focus"

– Peter Doolittle

What is it?

Working memory is the ability to hold information in your mind long enough to use it. Think of it like a Post-it note that is used to remember information for a short period of time. It has a limited capacity and although there will be variations in the working memory capacity of young children, a typical five-year-old child may be expected to handle just two or three 'chunks' of information. When we talk about 'chunks', we're referring to meaningful units of information that can be stored and manipulated in working memory. For example, a chunk could be a digit, a word, a syllable or a simple concept.

Why is it important?

Working memory is fundamental to following instructions and problem-solving. It provides a strong foundation for a variety of cognitive and social skills. Interestingly, there appears to be a positive relationship between working memory and attention, and working memory and mathematics (Gathercole & Packiam Alloway, 2008). This is not surprising when you consider it's the part of memory responsible for taking the pieces of selected information and temporarily holding and manipulating it in order to solve a multistep maths problem. Individuals with larger working memory capacities can hold more numbers in mind and perform calculations more efficiently without external aids. In a similar way, working memory is critical when learning to read from decoding individual words to comprehending and synthesising information from entire texts.

What is happening in the brain?

When a young child uses their working memory skills, their brain is actively engaging multiple regions and processes to hold and manipulate information temporarily. This involves the prefrontal cortex, parietal cortex, hippocampus and a network of neural connections that become stronger with practice. Attention control and the release of dopamine also contribute to the effective use of working memory.

Behaviour

When a child is having difficulty with their working memory, you are likely to see these sorts of behaviours:

- Difficulty remembering instructions
- Difficulty following multistep directions
- Difficulty recalling rules to a game
- Difficulty remembering what was happening before a distraction or break
- Difficulty remembering a storyline over consecutive days

Working memory in action

A group of five-year-olds eagerly gathers around a table where a memory game is set up. The educator, Emma, explains the rules of the game, holding up a set of colourful cards with pictures of animals, shapes and objects.

"Today we're going to play a fun memory game," Emma announces enthusiastically. "Each of these cards has a matching pair hidden somewhere among them. Your challenge is to find the matching pairs by turning over two cards at a time. But here's the twist: you need to remember where each card is located, because you can only turn over two cards at a time. Are you ready to use your memory skills and have some fun?"

The children nod eagerly and they gather closer around the table, eager to begin the game. The educator demonstrates how to play by flipping over two cards to reveal their images: a red apple and a green apple. "They are both apples," says Mia, "but they are not the same colour, so they don't match."

The next turn goes to Lucas, who turns over two trains. "Let's see if these two cards match," Emma says, encouraging the children to pay close attention. After a thorough comparison of the pictures, everyone agrees they look the same and are, therefore, a match.

As the children take turns flipping over pairs of cards, they carefully observe the images and use their working memory to remember the locations of the cards they've seen before. With each turn, they concentrate intently, try to recall where the matching pairs might be hidden and plan their next move.

Cognitive Load Theory

Cognitive Load Theory is an important concept to understand because it can help to guide you in how to design activities and present information to young children in a way that supports their learning and development. Think back to an occasion when you were in the position of a learner, for example, learning to drive, learning a new language or coordinating dance steps and arm movements in the gym. How did it feel? Most probably a bit overwhelming. In such situations our brain has to work hard to remember particular sequences or sounds and this requires it to use a lot of energy, so it's no wonder that we feel exhausted at the end of a session.

Basically, Cognitive Load Theory is about how much mental effort we need to use when we are learning something new or doing an activity we haven't mastered yet. Just like adults, children have a limit to how much information they can take in and process at once. When there is too much information, or tasks are too complicated, it can be harder for children to learn effectively. As the educator, it is therefore your responsibility to manage the cognitive load – once again, we can relate it back to Vygotsky's ZPD. This time, though, think of it in terms of the *amount* of information you are giving children – too much is overwhelming. When thinking about our working memories, using a metaphor such as a cup might be helpful – if you keep pouring liquid into it once it's full, it will overflow. There is a limit to how much it can hold, so be aware!

How can working memory be enhanced?

First and foremost, be proactive and anticipate where children are likely to encounter difficulties learning new information. This requires 'task analysis' and involves looking at experiences from a cognitive perspective and working out which executive functions are going to be needed to complete it (the template 'Planning an experience through the SOWATT lens' on page 122 will help you). Once you have thought about this, you are then more able to use some strategies that can help build children's working memory and, at the same time, prevent meltdowns as a result of frustration. Another way to think about it, is lowering the barriers to learning, not the bar.

Chunking information

Part of getting to know each child is knowing their ZPD. Breaking tasks and information into smaller, more manageable pieces may help some children access it more easily. For example, instead of presenting a long list of instructions all at once, break them down into smaller steps. This helps reduce the cognitive load and makes it easier for children to understand and remember. It could be as simple as reducing the steps necessary to go out to play to single words: "Hat, bottle, door", or reminding children how you want them to sit: "Mat, bottom, pretzel, thanks!"

Clear instructions and modelling

Provide clear and simple instructions, and demonstrate tasks whenever possible. Visual aids, such as pictures, diagrams or demonstrations, can also be helpful for young children to understand new concepts.

Use multisensory approaches

We gather information through our senses. The more senses we engage, the more likely information will stick. For example, incorporate hands-on activities, music, movement and interactive experiences to make learning more engaging and memorable. Using think alouds or narrating tasks alongside actions is another helpful way of supporting children to remember something.

Priming

Priming for learning involves preparing the brain to absorb new information more effectively. This technique leverages the brain's ability to recognise and recall previously encountered stimuli, making it easier to learn and remember new content. In your classroom, priming can be especially beneficial, as it sets the stage for young children to engage with new concepts and skills.

Provide scaffolded support

Offer support and guidance as children learn new skills, gradually removing scaffolds as they become more proficient. This helps prevent children from feeling overwhelmed and builds their confidence and independence over time.

Menu of activities

Below is a menu of example activities that can be used to foster working memory. Choose one or two to get you started and ask yourself: "How can I make the activity easier/harder and hit the ZPD?"

Figure 9: Example activities to foster working memory

Working memory			
Play "I went to market and bought…"	Find the matching pair games	Play card games: Uno, Snap, Go Fish	Play "What's in the box?" (20 questions)
Play Happy Families	Sort objects into categories	Play board games: Snakes & Ladders	Play "I Spy"
Play Kim's Game	Imaginative play requiring different roles	Play Dominoes	Scavenger Hunt
Play "Who am I?"	Echo rhythms	Retell stories remembering sequence of events or characters	Play a xylophone – using coloured notation
Play Sound Bingo	Action games	Create or replicate patterns with a range of materials	Play Jump in the Hoop

Language to support the development of working memory

Most of the examples provided here relate to conversations that might take place before the start of an activity. Priming the brain in this way is helpful in making connections to prior learning. When children realise they have done something like this before, it reduces potential stress and, ultimately, the cognitive load.

Asking children to articulate instructions before starting activities provides a useful check for educators that children have understood what they are required to do. By putting the instructions into their own words, children can clarify any confusion they may have and confirm their understanding of what is expected of them. Paraphrasing in this way requires children to actively engage with the instructions, and this can enhance memory encoding. When children rephrase the instructions in their own words, they are more likely to remember them accurately because they have processed the information more deeply. They are also more likely to retain the information in their working memory, making it easier for them to recall and follow the instructions as they work on the task.

Table 4: Language that supports the development of working memory

Working memory
"What is your favourite part of the story and why?"
"What have you discovered so far?"
"Is all the information here, or do we need to look elsewhere?"
"From our previous experience, where else might we find what we need?"
"What kind of task is this; have we done anything like this before?"
"Do you remember when we read the story last week about the girls on the swing? Is this story anything like that one?"
"What do I have to do?"
Practise self-talk: "I wonder where this piece will go, it's got a curved side."

TIPs:

- Model self-talk; verbalisation of the task.
- Work on visualisation skills.
- Chunk information into smaller bites – limit/simplify instructions.
- Have a child teach *you*.
- Make tasks multisensory – present verbal and pictorial information simultaneously.
- Play games with a memory element.
- Label groups of ideas and concepts – this is useful for later retrieval.
- Summarise learning at regular intervals throughout the day.
- Do not model a whole task at once; support the process one or two steps at a time.
- Accompany modelling with verbalisation – say what you, the educator, is doing, out loud.
- Use verbal rehearsal as much as possible.
- Teach the children that our brain is like a computer, in that we store things in mental files.
- Provide opportunities to talk about the day ahead and reflect on what children did throughout the day.
- Help make connections to prior learning.

Chapter 6

Attention

"You learn something every day if you pay attention"

– Ray LeBlond

What is it?

It is generally accepted that there are three related, yet distinct, processes of **attention**:

alerting, *orientating* and *sustained*

These interact with one another and can occur simultaneously or in succession.

Why is it important?

Attention is foundational for all the other elements in the SOWATT framework and may be the source of common variance in performance across executive function tasks (Posner & Rothbart, 2007). Attentional skills not only play an important role in learning, but also in social skills because they contribute to the ability to maintain focus during interactions, filter irrelevant information and focus on social cues. The ability to sustain attention over a period of time is sometimes referred to as 'executive' attention. Without it, tasks don't get finished and children don't get the sense of achievement that comes from completion of an activity.

What is happening in the brain?

When a young child uses their attention skills, several key processes are happening in their brain. The reticular activating system – a network of neurons in the brainstem – helps regulate arousal and alertness. It keeps the brain awake and ready to pay attention to important stimuli, ensuring the child is alert and focused. The anterior cingulate cortex located near the middle of the brain monitors performance and detects errors. It helps children stay on task by noticing when their attention is wandering, and redirecting their focus back to the task. Effective attention involves communication between these brain regions and the prefrontal cortex. They need to work together as a network to help children focus and sustain attention.

When a task is completed successfully, it provides a sense of achievement and satisfaction. The brain interprets this accomplishment as a positive outcome and releases dopamine as a reward, reinforcing the behaviour associated with task completion. This encourages us to repeat the behaviour that led to the reward, increasing motivation to engage in similar tasks in the future and ultimately help us reach our goals.

Behaviour

When a child is having difficulty with their attention, you are likely to see these sorts of behaviours:

- Little or no engagement with a task
- Easily distractable – unable to filter out distractions

- Excessive daydreaming
- Giving up on tasks not long after starting them
- Giving responses to questions that are completely off-topic
- Wandering aimlessly around the room
- Looking for distractions – either something or someone
- Fidgeting or restlessness
- Forgetfulness
- Inconsistent performance

Attention in action

Children are gathered around a large, colourful rug where the educator, Zac, explains that they will be playing a game called Mystery Box.

"All right, friends, are you ready for a fun game?" Zac asks. "I have a special box here with some mystery objects inside. One at a time, each of you will reach into the box without looking and feel the object inside. Then, you'll take turns describing what you feel to the rest of the group. But here's the catch: you need to listen carefully to your friends' descriptions because you'll have to guess what the mystery object is based on their clues. Are you ready to use your attention skills and have some fun?"

The children nod eagerly and await their turn. With a sense of anticipation, the first child reaches into the box and carefully feels the object hidden inside. "It's smooth and round and has a little stick coming out of the top of it," Chelsea announces, describing the object to the group. "And it feels cold!"

The other children listen intently, their attention focused on the description of the mystery object. After considering the clues, one child raises their hand excitedly. "I think it's an apple!" exclaims Ted.

The first child nods with a smile as Zac reveals the object – a shiny red apple. The group erupts into cheers and applause, celebrating the correct guess. As the game continues, each child takes turns reaching into the mystery box, describing the objects they feel, and guessing their identity based on their classmates' clues. The children concentrate intently, using their attention skills to listen carefully to the descriptions and recall details about the objects.

With each new round, the children become more engaged and focused, eagerly anticipating their turn to participate and cheering on their friends as they make guesses and uncover the mystery objects.

How is attention enhanced?

Our attention is pulled in so many different directions at a time. Our brains not only have to focus, but simultaneously filter out irrelevant information. Apparently, when we are reading, our minds typically wander anywhere from 20-40% of the time (AGDE, 2022). Voluntarily keeping our attention on one thing continuously takes a lot of effort.

As an educator, it is very important to remember that a child's brain (and also an adult's) is always paying attention – but maybe not to the thing(s) that you want it to! It is also worth remembering that the brain needs a lot of energy to work efficiently, and therefore looks for patterns as a way to efficiently process information and reduce energy expenditure. By recognising patterns, the brain can quickly categorise and make sense of incoming information without having to analyse each individual piece of data separately.

Once a pattern is identified, the brain can predict what is likely to happen next based on previous experiences or knowledge of similar patterns. This predictive processing allows the brain to allocate resources more selectively. When familiar patterns are detected, the brain can activate automated, or habitual, responses without the need for conscious effort or deliberation. These automatic responses are more energy-efficient than deliberate, effortful processing, allowing the brain to conserve energy for other tasks. This sounds well and good, provided our focus is on the right thing!

A word about distractions

Distractions are everywhere and classrooms certainly have their fair share of them. Since we learn through our senses, distractions take many forms: visual, audio, tactile and even environmental, such as classroom temperature and lighting. An awareness of potential distractors is particularly important for the educator with children displaying ADHD traits. Such children really struggle with these distractors – the filtering ability of their brains is less effective and that's why they can't focus for long on a single task.

However, distractions are not all bad. Keeping our attention on one thing requires the brain to use a lot of energy – it is tiring. Studies have shown that, in fact, daydreaming is not as bad as we first thought (Doebel, 2020). It can be like a rebooting of the attention system!

A child's attention may be affected by:

Alertness – refers to a child's state of mind. It can be too alert, as in the case of children with ADHD, or unresponsive, for example, when a child is tired. A classroom that is too warm is likely to make children drowsy and sluggish, and one that is too cold becomes a distraction as children look for ways to keep warm. Listen out for rumbling tummies, as hunger can be another unwanted distractor.

Another factor contributing to a child's level of alertness is their emotional state. A child who is missing their mum and feeling sad is unlikely to want to engage with their peers; similarly, children will readily disengage if they are bored. On the other hand, an overexcited child looking forward to their birthday party at the end of the day can also struggle to focus their attention, particularly in large-group, sedate activities such as circle time. Being aware of and addressing children's emotional state before expecting them to engage in such activities may help to aid their attention and prevent their emotions being a distraction for their peers.

Orientation – refers to the focus of the attention. It's the child turning their head and fixing their eyes on the educator in response to the words, "Look at this."

Before a child can make memories or learn, you must capture their attention. Each time a child focuses their attention, neuronal circuits become stronger and more efficient at carrying new data into storage.

Fortunately, there are a few tried and tested ways of getting children back on track when their attention has wandered. They involve: **colour, movement, sounds, touch** and **curiosity**.

Colour: Bright and vibrant colours tend to attract young children's attention because they are visually stimulating. Colourful objects or materials can draw children's focus and engage their interest, making learning experiences more enjoyable and memorable.

Movement: Young children are naturally drawn to movement. Dynamic and interactive activities that involve movement, such as dancing, playing games or hands-on exploration, can capture their attention and keep them engaged for longer periods. Movement also helps to stimulate various sensory experiences, enhancing learning and cognitive development. As mentioned earlier, the brain likes to make predictions based on previous patterns; therefore, by changing the expected movement, you can reset the attention filter.

Sounds: Children are highly responsive to auditory stimuli, and sounds can have a powerful impact on their attention. Music, rhymes, storytelling and other auditory experiences can captivate children's interest and facilitate learning. Something I have seen used to good effect is 'the singing bell', which produces a sustained note with a single strike. Sounds can also help to create a multisensory learning environment when combined with other stimuli, such as visuals or movement.

Touch: Don't underestimate a gentle touch to a shoulder or arm to refocus behaviour. This non-verbal action acts as a cue to let a child know that you've seen what they are doing and that they need to refocus their

attention on what you are expecting them to do, rather than what they are currently doing.

Curiosity: This is a fundamental driving force behind children's learning and exploration. Young children are naturally curious about the world around them and seek out new experiences to satisfy their curiosity. Curiosity motivates children to pay attention, ask questions and actively participate in learning activities.

Sustained or executive attention

In young children, the development of sustained or executive attention undergoes significant growth during early childhood and is influenced by various factors, including neurological maturation, environmental experiences and social interactions. Activities that promote the development of executive attention in young children may include structured play, interactive games, puzzles, storytelling and guided activities that require sustained engagement, such as mindfulness.

Mindful walks are a good way to encourage children to focus on their surroundings, including sights, sounds and sensations. By paying close attention to details, such as the colour of leaves, the sound of birds or the feel of the ground beneath their feet, children practise sustaining their attention on specific stimuli, which strengthens their overall ability to concentrate. On mindful walks, children are guided to notice when their minds wander and gently bring their focus back to the present moment. This practice helps them become more aware of distractions and improves their ability to redirect their attention, a skill that is beneficial in academic settings and daily activities. Engaging multiple senses during a mindful walk (sight, sound, touch, smell) can help children develop a richer sensory vocabulary and a heightened awareness of their environment. This sensory engagement is critical for developing attentional control, as it requires noticing and distinguishing between different sensory inputs. The slow and deliberate pace of a mindful walk can teach children patience and the ability to stay calm. These qualities are essential for maintaining attention, particularly in situations that require sustained focus or involve waiting.

When children are encouraged to explore their environment mindfully, they develop a sense of curiosity and interest. This intrinsic motivation to learn about their surroundings can translate into a greater willingness to engage with and attend to new information in other contexts, such as the classroom. Spending time in nature has been shown to reduce stress and improve executive function and self-regulation. The natural environment provides a varied and sensory-rich experience that can be more engaging and less overstimulating than indoor settings, which really helps children to practise and sustain their attentional focus.

Menu of activities

The menu opposite provides some examples of activities that can be used to foster children's attention. Choose one or two to get you started and ask yourself: "How can I make the activity easier/harder and hit the ZPD?"

Figure 10: Example activities to foster attention

Attention			
Look for patterns in nature	Tracing activities	Imaginative play	Look at books requiring children to look for something specific, such as *Where's Wally?*
Observational drawings	Feely bag activities	Go on a sensory walk	Clapping rhythms
Play games like Spot the Difference	Action songs – such as Head, Shoulders, Knees and Toes	Card games like Snap	Pass and catch an imaginary ball in a group
Jigsaw puzzles	Mirror partner work – one person mirrors the other	Follow the Leader	Look at pictures to make predictions
Play Spot It	Play Musical Statues	Complete mazes	Read stories that require audience participation, such as sound effects

Language to support the development of attentional skills

Conversations to support the development of attention need to occur before, during and after activities. For obvious reasons, children's attention needs to be tuned in before starting an activity.

Table 5: Language that supports the development of attentional skills

Attention
"Be sure to listen, so you know what to do."
"I am going to say something very important, so your attention needs to be on me and not on anything else."
"How do I know you are really listening?"
"What do we have to do to show people we are listening?"
"I see you are looking carefully... that's what we call attention."
"Stop and look carefully at what you are doing."
"Point to the words that tell you that."
"Why do we need to look so carefully?"
Ask children to check whether they are looking/listening to begin with and then remind them to check that they are continuing to focus as they go along.
Draw children's attention to stimuli using precise language: at the top, bottom, in the middle, by the side of..., front, back, left, right.
When completing a jigsaw, ask, "When you compare the pieces with the picture on the cover, can you see where the sky is and where the trees are and what is at the bottom of the picture?"
"I think you pay attention better when we put the toys we don't need out of sight. Then you won't be distracted by them."
"If there is a distraction, then I will ignore it."
"Did you notice that the snowman has a small circle for its head, then a bigger one for its chest and then a really big one for the bottom? Do you see how it gets bigger and bigger each time?"
"How could we work together to solve this?"

TIPs:

- Model the need to look/listen and explain what being ready to learn looks and feels like.
- Teach active listening – what does it look like? Use lips and ear cards initially.
- Ensure children are attending to what you want them to.
- Use curiosity to promote attention.
- Reduce distractions in the environment where and when possible.
- Enlarge prints or pictures if sharing with a group.
- Ensure the physical environment is conducive for purpose: good lighting, furniture the correct size and the temperature is appropriate.
- Be aware that a child might be sleep deprived.
- Develop checking behaviour with questions such as, "Do you have the glue and all the other things you need?"
- Work on building the skill of comparing, for example, take two pictures or objects and ask, "What's the same/different about them?"
- Make deliberate mistakes when reading a well-known story – children love correcting the teacher!
- Take movement breaks.
- Practise mindfulness: engage in mindfulness or meditation exercises to train the mind to stay present and focused.
- Introduce the idea of a 'learning friend', i.e. someone you sit next to when you don't want to be distracted.

Chapter 7

Thinking flexibly

"If you don't like something, change it; if you can't change it, change the way you think about it"

– Mary Engelbreit

What is it?

Thinking flexibly is the ability to be able to change perspectives, generate alternative solutions and consider options.

Why is it important?

Children who are more flexible in their thinking are better able to adapt to new situations, solve problems creatively and thrive in an ever-changing world. Cognitive flexibility is also important in social interactions, as it enables children to understand and respond to the perspectives and intentions of others, and resolve conflict.

What is happening in the brain?

When a young child uses their flexible thinking skills, their brain is actively engaging multiple regions and processes. The prefrontal cortex, anterior cingulate cortex, basal ganglia and parietal cortex all play important roles, along with the release of dopamine and the strengthening of neural connections through synaptic plasticity. These combined efforts help children adapt their thinking, switch between tasks and approach problems in new ways.

Behaviour

When a child is having difficulty with their cognitive flexibility, you are likely to see these sorts of behaviours:

- Difficulty coping with changes in routine or a different educator
- Difficultly switching focus from one task to another
- Difficulty seeing something from someone else's perspective
- Difficulty improvising when things don't go as expected
- Difficulty accepting that there can be exceptions to rules
- Difficulty changing a negative mindset and 'moving on'
- Having a fixed mindset – children make up their mind about something and that's the way it is!

Thinking flexibly in action

Three children are engaged in a cooperative block-building activity. They are tasked with building a structure using a variety of building materials, including wooden blocks, cardboard tubes and plastic connectors. As they work together, the children encounter challenges and obstacles that require them to think flexibly and adapt their plans. For example, they may need to adjust their design if it becomes unstable or if they run out of certain materials. Additionally, they must collaborate with their peers, listen to different ideas and be open to alternative approaches to

problem-solving. Through this play-based activity, the children practise cognitive flexibility by exploring multiple solutions, adjusting their strategies and working collaboratively to achieve their goal.

How is thinking flexibly enhanced?

Play-based learning: Play is a natural and effective way for children to develop cognitive flexibility. Through imaginative play, children engage in scenarios that require them to switch roles, perspectives and rules. For example, playing 'pretend' allows children to take on different roles and problem-solve in diverse contexts.

Exposure to novelty: Introducing children to new and diverse experiences helps expand their thinking and encourages them to consider multiple perspectives. This could include exposure to different cultures, environments, foods or activities that challenge their existing schemas and encourage cognitive flexibility.

Open-ended activities: Providing opportunities for open-ended activities and exploration allows children to practise generating multiple solutions to a problem. Activities such as building with blocks, creating art or engaging in sensory play encourage children to experiment, innovate and adapt their approaches as needed.

Encouraging exploration: Encouraging children to explore and experiment with materials and ideas fosters cognitive flexibility. Provide a variety of materials and resources for children to manipulate and use creatively, allowing them to generate their own solutions and adapt their thinking based on their discoveries.

Problem-solving challenges: Presenting children with age-appropriate problem-solving challenges encourages them to think flexibly and consider alternative approaches. These challenges can range from simple puzzles to more complex tasks that require planning, reasoning and persistence.

Modelling flexibility: Model cognitive flexibility by demonstrating openness to new ideas, willingness to consider alternative perspectives and adaptability in problem-solving situations. Children learn from observing how adults approach challenges and navigate unfamiliar situations; it might be as simple as changing the way that children line up or sit on the mat.

Encouraging perspective-taking: When children are encouraged to consider others' viewpoints and feelings, it helps them develop cognitive flexibility. Activities that promote empathy, such as storytelling, role playing or discussions about characters' perspectives in books, help children understand that there are multiple ways of seeing the world.

Gradual challenges: Providing challenges that are slightly beyond children's current abilities but are still achievable encourages them to stretch their thinking and develop cognitive flexibility. Gradually increasing the complexity of tasks allows children to build confidence in their problem-solving abilities while expanding their cognitive skills. Alongside this, teach children about a 'growth mindset' – the belief that they can get better at something through practice and effort. If they struggle with something, instead of thinking, "I'm just not good at this", they change their mindset to, "I'm not good at doing this … yet! I can improve with more practice." This way of thinking helps them keep trying and learning from mistakes.

Teaching 'popsicle and pipe-cleaner thinking'

In my experience, children love learning about their brain. They are fascinated when you tell them that every time you learn something new their brain grows! One way of introducing them to their brain is to say that their brain is like a special control centre inside their head that helps them think, learn and feel things. Emphasise that they have the power to control and take care of their brains, just like they take care of other parts of their bodies. Provide examples to illustrate how they can take charge of their brains. For instance, explain that when they choose to pay attention in class or try to solve a puzzle, they are using their brains in a positive way.

Talk about how the choices they make can affect their brains. Explain that doing things like eating healthy food, getting enough sleep and practising positive thinking can help their brains grow strong and healthy.

When it comes to developing flexible thinking, try introducing them to 'popsicle and pipe-cleaner thinking'. Have props ready to show the differences between the two items. Demonstrate the rigidity of the popsicle stick. When we use popsicle thinking, it is in situations that need order, organisation and logical reasoning. It is valuable for tasks that require careful planning, attention to detail and adherence to established procedures. Used in this way it can build confidence in tackling structured tasks.

Pipe-cleaner thinking, on the other hand, is characterised by flexibility, creativity and openness to new ideas. It encourages children to explore multiple perspectives, think outside the box, and embrace ambiguity and uncertainty. This style of thinking is conducive to creativity, innovation and originality. Teaching children pipe-cleaner thinking empowers them to generate creative solutions, adapt to changing situations, and approach problems with curiosity and imagination. It is really handy in conflict situations when, for example, another child has the toy they want. Instead of having a meltdown, they can apply their pipe-cleaner thinking to solve the problem.

Teaching popsicle and pipe-cleaner thinking is not only good for problem-solving situations. It can be used with children who are perfectionists or risk-averse, and encourage them to step out of their comfort zone. It may also be applied to situations requiring something non-negotiable, such as listening to the teacher and packing up. It encourages collaboration, communication and empathy as children learn to consider and respect diverse perspectives. Moreover, it nurtures self-confidence and self-efficacy as children realise their capacity to overcome obstacles and make meaningful contributions through their creative ideas and thoughtful problem-solving approaches.

Menu of activities

The below menu provides some examples of activities that can be used to foster children's flexible thinking. Choose one or two to get you started and ask yourself: "How can I make the activity easier/harder and hit the ZPD?"

Figure 11: Example activities to foster flexible thinking

Thinking flexibly			
Have fun with opposites	Tell jokes – particularly ones that play on words	Group toys or objects in different ways – buttons are good for this activity	Change the rules to well-known games
Teach pipe-cleaner and popsicle thinking	5 Matchsticks: Make a pattern, draw it, make a different one, draw, repeat – wrapping paper may be created	Have fun with rhymes	Play-Doh – "What can you make with one lump?"
Complete mazes	Imaginative play/ puppet theatre	Provide opportunities for open-ended problem-solving	Encourage problem-solving behaviour
Thumbprint/ Squiggle Art	Suggest alternative endings to favourite stories	Craft activities – same materials, different outcomes	Play the Hoop game
Partner drawings	Look at optical illusions	What can you make from a cardboard roll?	Construction with Magna-Tiles/Lego

Language to support the development of flexible thinking skills

Table 6: Language that supports the development of flexible thinking skills

Thinking flexibly
"Can you think of another way of doing this?"
"What do you think might work?"
"What options do you have for getting unstuck?"
"Why is this one better than that one?"
"How is _____ different from _____?"
"What do you think will happen if…?"
"How else might you be able to group them?"
When completing a jigsaw, say, "Look, now you are comparing the colour, then you can look at the shape."
When looking at pictures of people in different situations, ask, "What do you think they are thinking?"
"Could there be more than one reason?"
"How do you think Jonathon will feel tomorrow when he comes back to Kinder?"
"Can you think how this will help us when we go to the zoo tomorrow?"
"What is the problem?"
"What if we didn't have any parks to go to? Then what would it be like?"
"I wonder how we can solve this. Do you have an idea?"
"I like Mia's idea, let's hear some other viewpoints on this."
"Can anyone else add to this idea?"
"I never thought about it that way."
"How could we work together to solve this?"

TIPs:

- Provide opportunities for more open-ended tasks which may generate more than one correct answer.
- Intentionally change the layout of the room once in a while.
- Share problem-solving strategies as a class and demonstrate there is often more than one way to achieve the correct answer.
- Model perspective taking.
- Provide opportunities for novelty – this requires the ability to think flexibly.
- Structure the environment so that children have opportunities to work with the teacher and different peers in different contexts.
- Promote a growth mindset and a 'have-a-go' attitude.

Chapter 8

Thinking about thinking

"We cannot solve our problems with the same thinking we used when we created them"

– Albert Einstein

What is it?

Metacognitive skills involve the ability to think about and regulate one's own thinking processes.

Why is it important?

Thinking about thinking is increasingly viewed as a pathway for facilitating children's understanding of when and how to apply strategies by enhancing their understanding, learning and agency. When we are aware of our thinking processes, we have greater control over how we use them. Thinking about thinking can be applied to all the other executive function skills to make them more effective.

I used to be the owner of a sports car that had an 'overdrive' function. This was used when the car was in top gear and motoring along, allowing the engine to operate more efficiently. Similarly, metacognition allows us to work more efficiently, because we are aware of our thinking and the strategies that had worked for us in the past. It supports us to monitor progress as we go along, instead of finishing a task and realising that we are completely off track. In essence, it helps to build self-awareness and puts the 'self' into self-regulation.

What is happening in the brain?

Effective thinking about thinking involves communication between several regions of the brain. The prefrontal cortex, anterior cingulate cortex, parietal cortex and hippocampus work together to help children monitor and evaluate their cognitive processes. The release of dopamine when children receive positive feedback strengthens neural connections through synaptic plasticity.

Behaviour

When a child is having difficulty with their metacognitive skills, you are likely to see these sorts of behaviours:

- Difficulties in self-regulation
- An episodic grasp of reality – they see each problem as a totally new experience and have an inability to link it to previous experiences
- Lacking the ability to generalise and transfer learning from one situation to another
- Lacking self-monitoring – difficulty monitoring their own progress or performance on tasks; they may not recognise when they are making mistakes or when they need to adjust their strategies
- Difficulty in setting goals – children may struggle to set goals for themselves or have unrealistic expectations about what they can achieve; they may lack a sense of direction or purpose in their learning activities

- Lack of reflection – they may not engage in reflective thinking about their own learning experiences; they may not think about what they have learned, how they learned it or what they could do differently next time
- Dependency on external guidance – they may rely heavily on external cues or guidance from adults rather than developing their own independent problem-solving and decision-making skills
- In social relationships, they show little evidence of the need to check their behaviour against others' responses
- Lacking self-awareness – they may struggle to evaluate their own learning or performance accurately; they may lack confidence in their abilities or have an inflated sense of their own competence

Thinking about thinking in action

Instead of just letting the children do whatever they want with the Magna-Tiles, today, Kim, the educator, wants them to practise their metacognitive skills. She says, "Today we are going to use our thinking brains in a special way – you are not only to build the tallest tower you possibly can, but I also want you to think about *how* you are going to do it and *how* you can work together. We're going to be thinking about how we think.

"Before you start building, talk with your friends about how you think you can make the tallest tower. How will you keep it from falling over? Discuss your plan and let me know what you decide."

A couple of minutes later, having shared their 'plan' with Kim, the children are eagerly rummaging through the tubs and selecting the tiles they think they are going to need.

To encourage the children to monitor their progress, Kim pops back to the group and says, "While you're building, use your attention to focus on what you're doing. Is your plan working? If not, why not? Talk about any changes you need to make."

Fifteen minutes later, following several collapses, a tower the height of a small child has risen from the mat. Kim returns and sits down on the mat to reflect with the children on how they managed to build such a tall tower that didn't fall over.

Marlow quickly responds with, "We had to change our plan because our tower kept falling, so we made the base wider."

"Yes, we had to use the bigger squares to build the base; these made it wider and stronger," adds Felix.

Maddy follows up with, "And we had to put each tile on very carefully and slowly when we got near the top so the tower wouldn't crash down. I had to stand on tiptoe."

Bit by bit, Kim gets the children to reflect on the strategies they used, and it soon becomes obvious that the children had indeed thought about their thinking, adjusted their plans and learned from their experience – just like smart builders do!

How is thinking about thinking enhanced?

Even young children have the capacity to reflect and think about their actions – practising it leads to improvement.

Reflection can occur in contexts that require children to detect challenges and pause, which in turn allows them to consider their options and control their responses. The challenge for educators is to create learning contexts that have the potential to trigger metacognitive processes in children. Metacognitive training encourages performance evaluation, including error detection and feedback processing.

Self-reflection: Encouraging children to reflect on their own experiences and learning processes is key to developing metacognition. You can prompt children to think about what they did, how they did it and what they learned from the experience. For example, after completing a puzzle, you can ask questions like, "How did you figure out where the pieces go?" and "What did you learn from doing this puzzle?"

Modelling metacognitive strategies: You can model metacognitive strategies by verbalising children's own thought processes during

problem-solving tasks. For instance, you might say, "I'm going to try this strategy to solve this problem. If it doesn't work, I'll try another approach." You can also slow down your thinking when evaluating something with, "Just a moment, let me think about that."

Explicit instruction: Providing explicit instruction on metacognitive strategies helps children become more aware of their own thinking processes. You can teach children specific strategies for planning, monitoring and evaluating their learning. For example, you might teach children how to make a plan before starting a task, monitor their progress as they work and reflect on their performance afterwards.

Encouraging goal setting: Helping children set goals for their learning encourages them to think about what they want to achieve and how they plan to accomplish it. You can work with children to set achievable goals and break them down into smaller steps. For example, a child might set a goal to learn how to write their name and create a plan for practising each letter.

Promoting problem-solving skills: Engaging children in problem-solving activities helps them develop metacognitive skills such as planning, monitoring and evaluating their strategies. You can provide opportunities for open-ended problem-solving tasks that require children to use trial and error, test hypotheses and revise their approaches based on feedback.

Encouraging discussion: Encouraging children to discuss their thinking with others promotes metacognition by providing opportunities for children to articulate their thoughts and reflect on their reasoning. You can facilitate group discussions where children share their ideas, ask questions and explain their thinking to their peers.

Creating a supportive environment: Creating a supportive environment where children feel comfortable taking risks and making mistakes is essential for fostering metacognition. Praising children's efforts and providing constructive feedback that focuses on the process rather than the outcome are also important strategies.

Menu of activities

The below menu provides some examples of activities that can be used to foster children's thinking about thinking. Choose one or two to get you started.

Figure 12: Example activities to foster thinking about thinking

	Thinking about thinking		
Circle time; ask: "What went well today?"	Talking about characters' actions in stories, ask: "What do you think they were thinking when…?"	Build towers and predict how high they can be built before they collapse; compare strategies for making them taller	Engage in conversations that provoke thinking about processes
Draw a reflection after a physical activity such as yoga	Mindful walking	Mindful minute	Mini interviews after an activity
Play back a video of the children playing and talk about what you see	Thumbs up, thumbs down for feedback on their effort/difficulty	Reflect on faces in a hand mirror; ask: "How can I make my face look happy, surprised, angry, etc.?"	Restorative chats
Reflect on problem-solving tasks; ask: "What could I do differently next time?"	Teach children how their minds are wired for growth	Help children see relationships between things/concepts	Mixing colours: explain how a particular shade was created and how it can be replicated

Language to support the development of thinking about thinking

Although many conversations are likely to be reflective in nature, there is merit in using metacognitive conversations to tune children into monitoring progress. Make sure these are used carefully, however, as there's nothing worse than being constantly interrupted when you are fully engaged in something.

Table 7: Language that supports the development of thinking about thinking

Thinking about thinking
"What makes you say that?"
"When have you done something like this before?"
"When is another time you needed to…?"
"Let's stop and look carefully at what you're doing."
"Yes, that's right, but how do you know it was right?"
"Why is this one better than that one?"
Ask questions about the child's thought processes – ask what they did and why.
"How did you know?"
"What might you do differently next time?"
"How did you do it last time?"
"What did you enjoy doing the most? Why?"
"Show me how you think." This requires children to stop and put their index finger on the side of their face in a thinking pose.
"You didn't think you could do that, and now look how well you did!"
"Show me the hard part."
"Just a moment, let me think about that."

TIPs:

- Model the behaviour – "That was a hard one! I had to think hard about that one, too."
- Give children the language of thinking – vocabulary and posing questions. Use think aloud strategies to demonstrate private speech.
- Set aside some reflection time in the day where children have the opportunity to think about something they enjoyed/went well/learned.
- Provide opportunities for children to explain how they did a particular task.
- Close your eyes and picture yourself back at the classroom door this morning. "How did you feel? What did you need to do first?"
- Teach the skill of monitoring progress, "How am I doing? What do I have to do next? Is there anything I don't understand?"
- Have visuals representing different moods – point to the picture that shows me how you felt today.
- Ask children to reflect on what they need to do in order to strengthen their ability to use goals/rules/regulate their behaviour.
- Give regular and specific feedback – not generic, "Good job", but rather, "I like the way you…"
- Teach self-questioning – "Where will this part go?"

Chapter 9

SOWATT's next?

"The way to get started is to quit talking and begin doing"
— Walt Disney

It should be clear by now that SOWATT isn't an 'add-on' to the curriculum; instead, it underpins everything you do. A focus on executive functioning does not take the place of the development of acquired skills such as early literacy and numeracy skills, rather, it sets the stage for them.

Play is the perfect medium to hone executive functions; it doesn't require large open spaces or expensive toys – it requires a combination of curiosity, imagination and experimentation (Resnick, 2017). This combination will stimulate children's thinking, requiring their executive functions to be challenged, and because activities in preschool are playful, children will want to engage in them and will, therefore, get the practice they need to cement strong skills.

Are you aware that in the 1960s NASA commissioned a test to identify and foster creative talent among NASA engineers and scientists? As part of the research, the study tested 1,600 children aged four to five years old. These same children were retested at ages 10 and 15, and then again as adults. They found that 98% of the four- to five-year-olds scored in the 'genius' category for creative thinking. However, by the time they were 10 years old, only 30% of the same children scored in the genius category. At age 15, the percentage dropped further to 12%. And among adults, only 2% retained their genius-level creative thinking. This suggests that creativity is an innate ability present in almost all children, but it can diminish due to external influences, such as educational and societal pressures. The study advocates for changes in educational practices to encourage and maintain creativity, critical thinking and divergent thinking skills throughout life and, you've guessed it: executive functions underpin these skills.

Mitchel Resnick, a professor at MIT and creator of the SCRATCH program, talks about the Creative Learning Spiral, as shown in Figure 13 below.

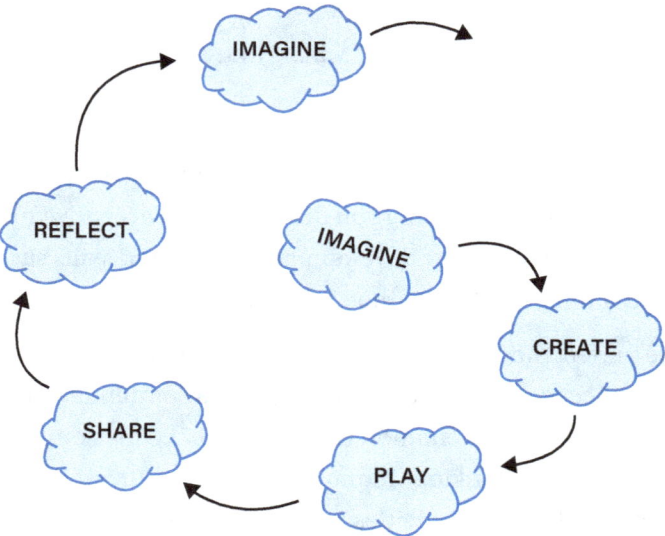

Figure 13: The Creative Learning Spiral

Reproduced with permission of Professor Mitchel Resnick (Resnick, 2017)

As young children play, they learn many things; they subconsciously learn about the creative process and begin to develop as creative thinkers. Reading about Professor Resnick's Creative Learning Spiral, I was struck by how important executive functions are to this model.

Imagine: This calls for the ability to set goals and *think flexibly*, to consider alternative ideas.

Create: In order to turn ideas into action you need to have *self-regulation*. You also need to *organise* your time and resources and pay *attention* to what's important without getting side-tracked. AND you need *working memory* to hold all the parts of the thinking.

Play: Children are constantly tinkering and experimenting with their creations. *Thinking flexibly*, paying *attention* and *working memory* are all important for this – a dose of *self-regulation* wouldn't go amiss either.

Share: Working collaboratively, listening to each other and building on each other's ideas relies on good *self-regulation*, controlling *inhibition* and keeping the goal in the *working memory*. It also requires the ability to *think flexibly* and consider other points of view.

Reflect: *Thinking about thinking* is a very important part in the learning process; it's how we learn from our mistakes and link new information with previous experiences.

Imagine: Based on their experiences going through the spiral, children imagine new ideas and new directions, and thus the process is repeated.

This Creative Learning Spiral is repeated over and over in Kinder. The materials vary (blocks, crayons, paper) and the creations vary (stories, drawings, songs). But the core process is the same.

If, as Professor Resnick says, "the Creative Learning Spiral is the engine of creative thinking", then executive functions might be likened to the spark plugs, pistons and valves that allow the engine to work. Using the SOWATT framework, you can identify the executive functions that are needed for each particular stage and task. This allows for them to be intentionally developed and for children to practise them in different contexts. As you will be aware by now, it is through repeated practice, in different contexts, with just the right amount of challenge that children can use their executive function skills and become creative thinkers both in Kinder and beyond.

To make it easier to implement SOWATT, it is recommended that you seek out the support of at least one colleague with whom you can work, share ideas and reflect about your experiences.

Having made the commitment to give it a go, the next step is to start planning. It is important to provide opportunities for children to apply their learning and introduce activities to support executive function development – hence the inclusion of the 'menus' with each of the SOWATT elements.

Start simple, use 'The classroom environment through the SOWATT lens' checklist provided on page 119 of the resources section to take a fresh look at your classroom set-up and reflect on the relationships you have with each child in your class. What are their strengths and weaknesses, and how do you know this?

Now start considering what can be done daily, weekly and regularly.

For example:

Daily:

- Model the behaviour you want to see.
- Make your own thinking explicit – use think alouds whenever possible.
- Scaffold or co-regulate experiences so children know what success feels like – use the menus provided in Chapters 3–8 to get you started.
- Play whole-class or large-group games that present varying degrees of cognitive challenge – see examples on page 128 of the resources section.
- Make time for reflection – it doesn't have to be long.
- Be aware of the language you are using – do less telling and provide more hints and cues, and try to extend children's thinking at every opportunity.
- Try a mindful activity – this does not have to take long, one minute is a good start and can be easily incorporated into the day, especially before or immediately after a transition. Encourage children to

be aware of their breathing by teaching techniques such as box breathing or shape breathing.
- Provide feedback to increase self-awareness.
- At storytime, intentionally focus on one or more executive function, for example, a character who displayed a particular trait.
- Be proactive, rather than reactive.

Weekly:

To start off, commit to intentionally planning for a minimum of **two small-group activities a day** which have been examined through the SOWATT framework – these can remain the same throughout the week.

It can be as simple as deciding that this week you are going to extend children's thinking as they play with the construction blocks. Decide which of the executive functions you want to target, for example, organisation, thinking flexibly and thinking about thinking. It is probably best not to try and do all six at the same time until you are familiar with them and can readily scaffold them through your interactions.

Using the planning templates on pages 120–124, write down the purpose of the activity from an executive function perspective and identify some of the language that you might use in your interactions with the children. Group these into Before, During and After stages of the activity. This does not mean you stay with the children throughout the experience, but you do need to touch base with them during their play, with the specific purpose of extending their thinking by questioning and giving specific feedback.

Afterwards, reflect on the activity with the children. This should happen as soon as possible after the activity due to the 'recency effect' – this is the fact that we tend to remember the most recent things we've done, and this is particularly true of young children. The end of the day is often too late for them to remember what they did before lunch, let alone remembering how they overcame a problem or organised their materials.

Remember to consider how you can make the experience more challenging. In the construction block scenario, it might involve setting the challenge to make a garage for 20 cars which you provide. Assuming the solution is a single-storey building, ask how they could adapt the garage to take up less floor space, yet accommodate the same number of cars. Let the children puzzle over a possible solution and observe their interactions – what does it tell you about particular children's executive functions and self-regulation? If no solution is forthcoming, don't provide one, just drop hints and cues such as reminding them about the type of car parks they see in the centre of a city.

You may consider sticking a small cue card (provided on page 121 of the resources section) alongside the activity with ticks in the boxes indicating the executive functions you are focusing on. This will serve as a reminder to all the adults in the room to intentionally use the appropriate language as they pass by the children at play. Taking a photo of the card alongside the children playing is also a good record of who engaged with activity and what the focus was. Remember to keep track of your ideas and experiences.

Regularly:

SOWATT is a framework for effective practices. Looking at your practice through an executive function lens will help you to work smarter, not harder!

Monitor the children's executive functions. Work with a colleague to observe and record what you see (use the checklists provided in the resources section to help guide these observations). Remember that children's executive functions need to be continually challenged in order to develop – work in the ZPD.

Some readers may be familiar with the term 'lethal mutation' – a phrase coined by Ed Haertel in the 1990s (Doebel, 2020), which relates to evidence-based practices being modified to such an extent that they are no longer effective. There is a fine line, therefore, between recognising the need for educator autonomy and the fidelity of an approach. One way to prevent 'lethal mutation' is for you to understand the principles that underpin the strategy or approach. It may be timely, therefore, to reread Chapter 2, which clearly lists the principles that underpin SOWATT. Without this knowledge and understanding, your practice is going to be less effective.

Finally, as you plan and create opportunities for your children to develop their executive function skills, please resist your classroom becoming like a primary school. I recently visited some preschool centres and was saddened to see children wearing hats with the slogan 'Getting ready for big school'. Early education is not simply a preparatory stop on the way to 'real' school, it *is* real learning and is building the foundations for future learning. It is a time when critical brain development is happening, when the foundational architecture for all that comes next is forming and strengthening.

YOUR classroom is where children begin to discover who they are, how the world works and what is possible. As educators and caretakers of your children's prefrontal lobes, the opportunities and experiences you provide will impact the development of critical life skills – executive functions; their development is just too important to be left to chance.

Chapter 10

Postscript to educators

This book was intended to help you in the classroom to support the development of executive functioning of every child who walks through your door. SOWATT is not a program to be followed prescriptively, it is a lens for you to look at your practice in a new light. It should most definitely not be viewed as 'an extra thing to do'. Rather, it should be embedded in play-based programs every single day.

SOWATT works best in the hands of creative educators who are stimulated by the challenges of educating the whole child – educators who practise the principles of good teaching and learning, and can adjust, adapt and apply information to suit the learning needs of *all* their students. Most likely you are already doing many of the things that are encouraged to enhance the development of executive function as discussed in this book. However, I hope that you now have a greater understanding of *why* a strategy you are using is effective, and an increased interest in targeting executive function development. Failing to intentionally develop executive functions in the preschool years is a missed opportunity.

YOU are a potential 'brain changer'. The environment you create and the experiences YOU plan and scaffold can change a child's developmental trajectory. Don't put it off until you think you have a better understanding or know all the answers; instead, use the space below to reflect on what you have learned from this book and ask yourself, "SOWATT can I do differently *today*, to improve my children's executive functioning?"

3 – 2 – 1

3 important takeaways from this book:

i)

ii)

iii)

2 things I can implement today:

i)

ii)

Share your reflections with at least **1** friend or colleague, to hold yourself accountable.

Resources

Learning outcomes linked to SOWATT	108
Executive function checklist: Junior Kinder	114
Executive function checklist: Senior Kinder	116
School readiness checklist for executive functions	118
The classroom environment through the SOWATT lens	119
Planning an experience through the SOWATT lens	120
Cue cards	121
Planning for executive functions	122
Planning for executive functions in the classroom	123
SOWATT weekly checklist	124
Listening and asking questions	125
Group games	128

Learning outcomes linked to SOWATT

Learning outcome 1	Link to SOWATT
Children have a strong sense of identity	O – knowing and following routines
	TT – developed sense of self-awareness
Children feel safe, secure and supported	S – joining in play
	TF – able to make decisions and choices
Children develop knowledgeable, confident self-identities and a positive sense of self-worth	S – working cooperatively, persisting and preserving in new or challenging tasks (emotional reg)
	O – sharing space and resources
Children develop their emerging autonomy, interdependence, resilience and agency	S – curbing impulsivity to talk over others
	TF – considering others' point of view, building empathy
Children learn to interact in relation to others with care, empathy and respect	S – emotional regulation, naming and recognising emotions
	TT – reflect on their actions and consider consequences for others
	TF/TT – display awareness of and respect for diverse cultures
	A – listen to others' opinions and points of view

Learning outcome 2	Link to SOWATT
Children are connected with and contribute to their world	**S, O, WM, TF** – cooperate with others and negotiate roles and relationships in play/group experiences
Children develop a sense of connectedness to groups and communities, and an understanding of their reciprocal rights and responsibilities as active and informed citizens	Contribute to decision-making and action, taking in matters that affect them
	Participate in reciprocal relationships
	TF – learn to 'read' the feelings and behaviours of others
	WM – begin to understand and use sustainable practices
Children respond to diversity with respect	**S, TF** – show respect for others
	WM, A, TT – become aware of connections, similarities and differences between people
Children become aware of fairness	Notice and react in positive ways to similarities and differences among people
	S, TF – treating people fairly
	TT, TF – consider and think critically about fair and unfair behaviour
	TT – understand and evaluate ways in which texts construct identities and create stereotypes
	TF – show empathy for those unfairly treated
Children become socially responsible and show respect for the environment	**S, WM, A, TF** – participate with others to identify and address environmental challenges and problems, and contribute to group ideas
	WM – learn and use Aboriginal or Torres Strait Islander names for land, local plants and animals, and the seasons
	S, O, WM, A, TF – explore, infer, predict and hypothesise in order to develop an increased understanding of the interdependence between land, people, plants and animals
	A – observe and describe elements of weather and changes in weather and climate

Learning outcome 3	Link to SOWATT
Children have a strong sense of wellbeing	S – remain accessible to others at times of distress, confusion and frustration
Children become strong in their social, emotional and mental wellbeing	S – increasingly cooperate and work collaboratively with others
	TT – recognise their individual efforts and achievements
Children become strong in their physical learning and wellbeing	S, O, TF – make choices, accept challenges, take considered risks, manage change and cope with frustrations and the unexpected
Children are aware of and develop strategies to support their own mental and physical health and personal safety	S – show an increasing capacity to understand, self-regulation and manage emotions
	TT – recognise the contributions they make to shared projects and experiences
	TT – recognise a range of emotions in themselves and others
	WM, A, TF – develop movement patterns, mobility and motor skills to manage and explore the physical environment
	S, A – use their sensory perceptions to explore and respond to the world
	S, O, WM, TT – manipulate equipment and manage tools with increasing competence and skill
	S, O, WM, TT – move to the tempo and rhythm of music
	S, O – negotiate play spaces to ensure the safety and wellbeing of others
	TT – recognise and communicate their body needs (for example, thirst, hunger, rest)
	S – build strategies to calm the body and mind
	TF – have agency and choice about their sleep and relaxation
	A, TT – notice and label feelings/emotions in themselves and others

Learning outcome 4	Link to SOWATT
Children are confident and involved learners	**S, WM** – share their ideas with others and ask questions of adults
Children develop a growth mindset and learning dispositions such as curiosity, cooperation, confidence, creativity, commitment, enthusiasm, persistence, imagination and reflexivity	**S, O, A, TF** – participate in a variety of rich and meaningful inquiry-based experiences

O, WM, TT – revisit previous learning experiences and plan new challenges

TT – talk about what is happening in their brain when they are learning new things |
| Children develop a range of learning and thinking skills and processes, such as problem-solving, inquiry, experimentation, hypothesising, researching and investigating

Children transfer and adapt what they have learned from one context to another

Children resource their own learning through connecting with people, place, technologies and natural and processed materials | **TF** – use trial and error to explore different possibilities through 'cause and effect'

O, WM, TF, TT – apply a range of thinking strategies to engage with situations and solve problems, and adapt these strategies to new situations

O, WM – create and use representation to organise, record and communicate mathematical ideas and concepts

O, WM, TF – explore their environment through asking questions, experimenting, investigating

TT – use reflective thinking to consider why things happen and what can be learned from these experiences

TF – develop and test theories to solve problems

O – use a range of strategies to organise mathematical thinking

S, O – engage with others to co-construct learning

WM – make connections between experiences, concepts and processes

S, O, WM, A, TF, TT – use the process of play, reflection and investigation to solve problems

TT – use strategies to reflect on and assess their learning and thinking |

Learning outcome 4	Link to SOWATT
	S, O, A – use their sense and body movements to explore natural and built materials and environments
	S, O, TF, TT – experience the benefits and pleasures of shared learning explorations, investigations and imaginary play scenarios
	S, O, WM, A, TF, TT – manipulate natural and manufactured materials and resources to investigate, take apart, assemble, invent and construct
	S, TF – explore ideas and theories using imagination, creativity and play
	O, WM, A, TT – use feedback from themselves and others to revise and build on an idea
	O, WM – retell simple stories using material or drama to represent ideas
	TF – explore 2D and 3D forms of expression to develop understandings of different artforms and elements

Learning outcome 5	Link to SOWATT
Children are effective communicators Children interact verbally and non-verbally with others for a range of purposes Children engage with a range of texts and gain meaning from these texts Children express ideas and make meaning using a range of media Children begin to understand how symbols and pattern systems work Children use digital technologies and media to access information, investigate ideas and represent their thinking	S – engage in enjoyable interactions using verbal and non-verbal language WM, A – listen to and act upon simple instructions O, WM – recount events from their lives S, O, WM, A, TF, TT – interact with others to explore ideas and concepts, clarify and challenge thinking, negotiate and share new understandings WM – demonstrate an increasing understanding of measurement and number using appropriate vocabulary A, WM – use language to communicate thinking about quantities to describe attributes of object and collection, and to explain mathematical ideas WM, TF, TT – begin to recognise the different sounds and begin to understand words in the community environment
	S, A – listen and respond to sounds and patterns in speech, stories and rhymes S, WM, A – sing and chant rhymes, jingles and songs WM – beginning to understand key literacy and numeracy concepts and processes TF – explore texts from a range of different perspectives O – retell simple stories in a logical sequence
	S, O, TF – use materials to create artworks A, TT – view, listen and respond to simple texts or music, and express how it makes them feel
	S, O, WM, A, TF, TT – begin to make connections between and see patterns in their feelings, ideas, words and actions, and those of others S, O – begin to sort, categorise, order and compare collections and events in their social and natural worlds
	S, WM – identify basic icons and keys, and use them to support their navigation

EYLF V2.0

Executive function checklist: Junior Kinder

		Semester One	Semester Two
	Self-regulation – the ability to control thoughts, emotions and actions, including curbing impulsivity and delaying instant gratification in favour of longer-term goals		
	Waits their turn in a game		
	Shares toys and resources		
	Listens to others		
	Follows the rules of a game		
	Aware of their personal space and that of others		
	Able to use simple words to express their feelings		
	Able to self-soothe		
	Able to control their emotions		
	Able to bounce back when things don't go their way		
	Able to curb impulsivity		
	Attempts to find solutions before seeking help		
	Initiates and maintains play with peers		
	Attempts to find solutions before seeking help		
	Separates easily from parents in the morning		
	Organisation – this involves goal setting and planning, organising resources, ideas and information		
	Knows and follows the routine at the start of the day		
	Beginning to take responsibility for personal belongings		
	Puts away bedding at the end of the rest period		
	Helps to pack up when asked		
	Can orientate a picture book correctly		
	Able to articulate what activity they want to do		
	Able to attempt simple tasks independently		
	Working memory – being able to hold information in your head long enough to use it		
	Able to follow a one-step instruction		
	Able to follow a two-step instruction		

		Semester One		Semester Two	
	Beginning to make connections between experiences				
	Demonstrating a developing vocabulary				
	Identifies simple patterns				
	Remembers simple rules when playing games				
	Can recall events correctly				
	Attention – the ability to focus on what is relevant in order to collect the relevant information to solve a problem or complete a task				
	Can complete tasks without getting distracted				
	Looks for and finds details in nature and pictures				
	Responds appropriately to cues from educators when they require attention				
	Can follow a story				
	Listens to peers				
	Thinking flexibly – being able to change perspectives, generate alternative solutions, consider options and cope with transitions and changes to routine				
	Displays curiosity towards new ideas				
	Can transition from one activity to another smoothly				
	Beginning to solve problems independently				
	Copes with changes to routines				
	Demonstrates an ability to play creatively				
	Demonstrates empathy towards peers				
	Thinking about thinking – being aware of your own thoughts, strategies, feelings and actions, and being able to monitor your progress				
	Recognises their strengths and areas where they may need more support/practice				
	Able to reflect on whether they enjoyed an activity				
	Able to recognise their emotions				
	Aware that their actions have consequences on others and themselves				
	Will ask for help when needed without becoming frustrated				

Key: Code according to frequency of behaviour observed

• Not observed   Infrequently demonstrated/when prompted   Usually/occasional reminders required   Independently

Executive function checklist: Senior Kinder

		Semester One	Semester Two
	Self-regulation – *the ability to control thoughts, emotions and actions, including curbing impulsivity and delaying instant gratification in favour of longer-term goals*		
	Waits their turn in a variety of situations		
	Plays cooperatively with others		
	Listens to others respectfully		
	Controls their behaviours and stays within the rules of the activity		
	Controls impulses, for example, calling out, interrupting, grabbing a toy		
	Perseveres when faced with unfamiliar and challenging situations		
	Regulates their emotions across a variety of contexts		
	Responds appropriately to emotion-related experiences		
	Organisation – *this involves goal setting and planning, organising resources, ideas and information*		
	Knows and is able to follow the daily routines		
	Takes responsibility for personal belongings		
	Finds and returns equipment in a timely and orderly manner		
	Able to articulate the steps needed to complete an activity		
	Knows that stories have a beginning, middle and end		
	Demonstrates planning behaviour, for example, being able to articulate what materials are needed and the steps involved to complete a craft activity		
	Working memory – *being able to hold information in your head long enough to use it*		
	Able to follow a three-step instruction		
	Remembers the rules to games		
	Able to retell a simple story and include some details, for example, names of characters		
	Follows conversations and able to add their own relevant comments/opinions		
	Asks relevant questions in class chats		

		Semester One		Semester Two	
	Makes connections between experiences and concepts				
	Uses appropriate vocabulary to describe objects, ideas and emotions				
	Identifies, continues and explains regular patterns				
	Attention – *the ability to focus on what is relevant in order to collect the relevant information to solve a problem or complete a task*				
	Sustains attention long enough to complete a task				
	Able to resist distractions				
	Notices details in nature, pictures and objects				
	Notices the feelings of others				
	Shows interest and curiosity in new experiences				
	Thinking flexibly – *Being able to change perspectives, generate alternative solutions, consider options and cope with transitions and changes to routine*				
	Applies a range of strategies to solve practical problems				
	Applies a range of strategies to solve social conflicts				
	Explores ideas using imaginative creativity and play				
	Able to cope with transitions				
	Able to cope with changes to routines				
	Willing to give new things a go				
	Demonstrates awareness of and respect for other children's ideas and opinions				
	Thinking about thinking – *being aware of your own thoughts, strategies, feelings and actions, and being able to monitor your progress*				
	Able to explain how they completed an experience or what they have learned				
	Recognises their individual efforts and achievements				
	Monitors progress and seeks help appropriately				
	Able to talk about and name their emotions				
	Aware of how their behaviour may affect others				

Key: Code according to frequency of behaviour observed

• Not observed   Infrequently demonstrated/ when prompted   Usually/occasional reminders required   Independently

School readiness checklist for executive functions

Self-regulation	Organisation	Working memory
Able to wait their turn when playing a game and not interrupting or speaking over someone	Able to follow the daily routines	Able to follow three-step instructions
Able to control impulses, for example, calling out, interrupting, grabbing a toy	Demonstrates responsibility for personal belongings	Able to remember the rules to games
Manages their emotions	Able to initiate tasks independently	Able to retell a simple story
Plays cooperatively with others	Can find and return equipment in an orderly manner	Follows conversations and is able to add their own relevant comments/opinions
Able to control their behaviours and stay within the rules of the activity	Able to articulate the steps they are going to take to complete an activity	
Able to manage frustration when they don't get what they want	Knows that stories have a beginning, middle and end	
Able to bounce back fairly quickly when they have been upset	Demonstrates planning behaviour, for example, by being to articulate what materials are needed to complete a craft activity	
Able to persevere when faced with unfamiliar and challenging learning situations		
Attention	**Thinking flexibly**	**Thinking about thinking**
Able to sustain attention long enough to complete tasks	Able to cope with changes to routine	Able to explain how they completed a task or what they have learned
Able to resist distractions	Able to cope with transitions	Is aware of own strengths and weaknesses
Notices details in nature, illustrations, toys, games	Able to solve simple social problems	Monitors progress and seeks help appropriately
	Able to solve simple practical problems	Able to talk about/name their emotions
	Demonstrates ability to play creatively	Is aware of how their behaviour affects others
	Able to recognise and respond appropriately to the feelings of others	
	Willing to give new things a go	

The classroom environment through the SOWATT lens

S
- Engage in positive and meaningful relationships with every child
- Build a sense of community and belonging
- Provide opportunities to promote children's agency
- Establish daily routines to reduce stress and anxiety
- Establish clear and consistent behaviour expectations and boundaries
- Praise the positive as much as possible
- Create an environment for children to feel safe to take a risk

O
- Provide clear scope and sequence of transitions
- Give 'time alerts' for packing up
- Ensure resources are organised, labelled and easily accessible
- Provide opportunities to plan together – model the process
- Encourage and foster routines

W
- Provide anchor charts/visuals as reminders of routines
- Be aware of the instructions you give, start simple and build in more steps and details
- Limit new information to allow for exploration

A
- Be aware of the temperature – too warm and children are sleepy
- Be aware of the noise level – are there some quiet areas?
- Pay attention to the language in the classroom – what are you hearing/saying?
- Look around the room and be aware of distractions – what are you going to do about them?
- How do you ensure that attention is being directed to you when you want it?
- Look for the positives in the children

T
- Change the physical layout from time to time to encourage children to be flexible
- Vary the routines from time to time, once children feel secure
- Provide opportunities for problem-solving
- Encourage curiosity
- Provide choice and some open-ended activities

T
- Make time for reflection during the day
- Check in with the children – ask them how they're going
- Ask children to explain their thinking – "What makes you say that?"

Planning an experience through the SOWATT lens

Executive function skills to be developed	What would you see/hear if executive function skill was developed?	What strategies will you use to help develop skill?
⏻		
✗		
⚙		
📣		
🎨		
💭		

Reflection	
How did it go?	What might you do differently next time?

Cue cards

Executive functions being targeted in this activity

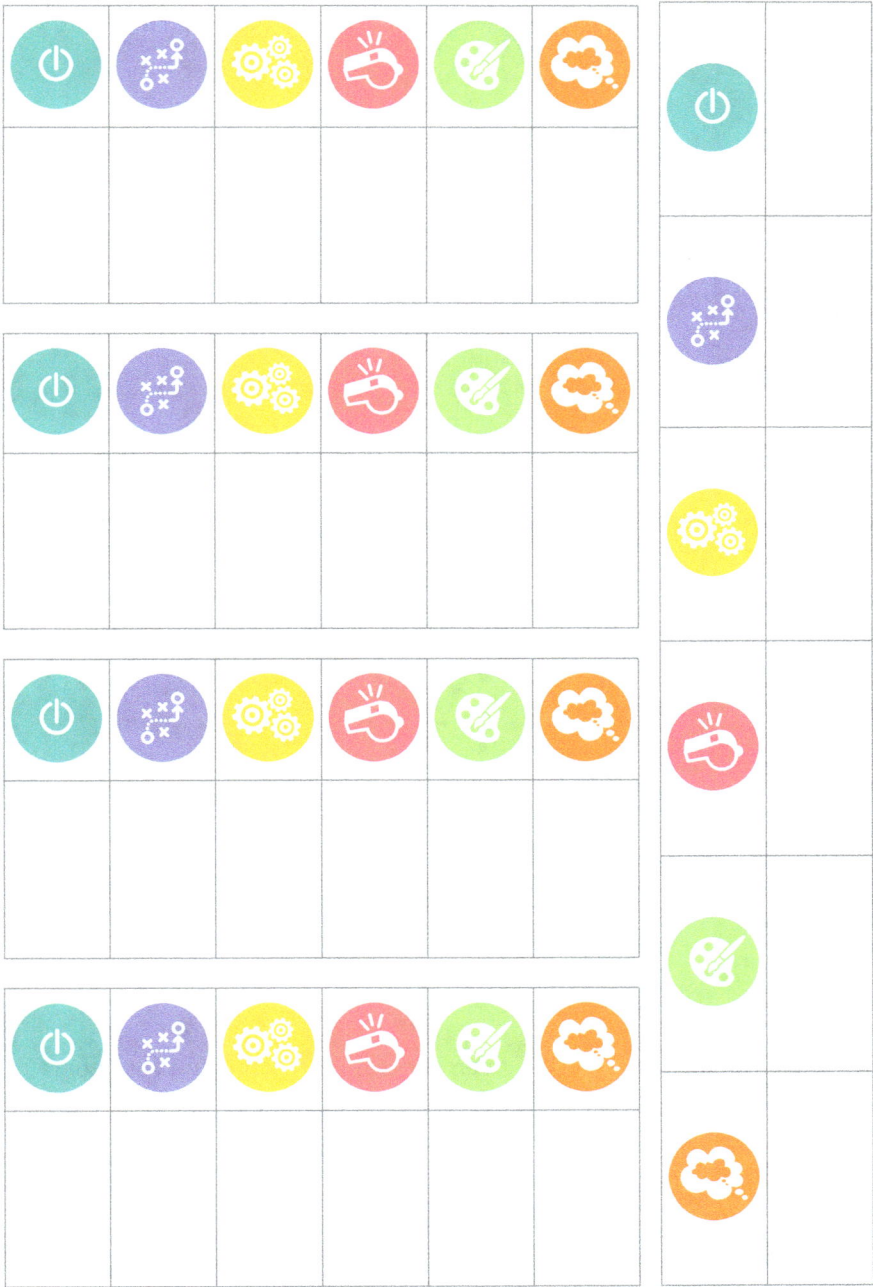

Planning for executive functions

What do you see as the priorities in your classroom?

What are you going to tackle first? Identify a **SMART** goal.

Identify the steps that need to be taken in order to achieve your goal:

What resources/support do you think you will need?

How will you know if you have been successful in achieving your goal?

Planning for executive functions in the classroom

Week beginning:

Activity/ experience	⏻	🧩	⚙️	🔔	🎨	💭	Observations

weekly checklist

Week beginning:

Class:

Executive function focus:

Try to plan for at least three activities that will intentionally enhance executive functions.

Strategies trialled					

Comments:

Listening and asking questions

The questions preschoolers ask play an important role in their cognitive development.

An easy way to remember basic dialogic strategies is to 'Follow the CAR'.

Follow the **CAR** stands for:

- **Follow** the child's lead
- **C**omment and *wait*
- **A**sk questions and *wait*
- **R**espond by adding a little more and *wait*

Try to ask open-ended questions to increase the level of thinking (cognition). Here are some examples to get you started:

During play:

- Tell me about what you are doing.
- What do you think of…?
- How do you know…?
- What does this remind you of?
- Which toy do you like playing with the most? Why?
- What else could we use this container for?

Problem-solving:

- Can you help me think this through?
- How could we work together to solve this?
- How did that happen?
- What do you think will happen if…?
- Can you think of a new way to do it?
- How could we make it work?
- What can we do to get it to work?

- How did you work that out?
- How did you get that to work?
- How do you know that?
- What did you notice?
- Do you have any other ideas?

At the end of an activity:

- How do you feel now you have finished?
- Tell me about what you built/made/created.
- What did you need to do to make this?
- What makes it work?
- Tell me about how you worked together.
- How are they alike/different?
- What do you think caused it to change?
- How might you do it differently next time?
- What do you like best about it?
- What was the hardest part and why?
- What problems did you have?
- What do you notice about...?
- Why did you choose... over...?
- What would have happened if there was/were...?
- What did you learn?

Reading books:

- Based on the cover of the book, what do you think is going to happen?
- What do you think will happen next?
- Who was your favourite character and why?
- What would you do if that was you?
- Would you want to be friends with...? Why?

- What did you notice happening?
- What happened at the beginning/middle/end?
- What do you think of the way the story ended?

Social/emotional questions:

- What three words do you think best describe you?
- What do you love doing that makes you happy?
- What do you know how to do that you could teach others?
- What is the most wonderful thing that has ever happened to you?
- What was the worst thing that has ever happened to you?

Source: Children's Questions: A Mechanism for Cognitive Development (Chouinard, 2007)

Group games

Games offer more than mere entertainment; they extend beyond developing physical skills and fitness. Every game, no matter how simple, serves as a framework through which children learn about themselves and others. Games act as mini societies, requiring children to make meaningful and valuable contributions. These contributions can range from adhering to the rules and putting in effort to making extraordinary efforts or setting aside personal needs for the benefit and success of the group. With guidance, games can surpass their role as entertainment and become instruments for fostering executive function development and nurturing emotionally intelligent, happy and purposeful children.

Remember to increase the cognitive challenge as children become more familiar with each game.

Red Light, Purple Light

Like in the popular children's game Red Light, Green Light, a teacher acts as a stoplight by standing at the opposite end of the room from the children and holding up different-coloured construction paper circles to represent stop and go. Children respond to specific colour cues (for example, purple is stop and orange is go) and then opposite cues (for example, purple is go and orange is stop), as well as to different shapes representing stop and go (for example, any colour circle is go and any colour square is stop).

The Freeze Game

Children dance when music plays and freeze when the teacher stops the music. Children dance slowly to slow songs and quickly to fast songs, alternating between different slow and fast songs. Children are then asked to respond to opposite cues: dancing quickly to slow songs and slowly to fast songs.

Colour-Matching Freeze

In this game, which is related to The Freeze Game, children dance when music is played and freeze when the music stops; however, children are asked to perform an additional step before freezing. Teachers tape different-coloured pieces of construction paper to mats placed on the ground. When the music stops, the teacher holds up a specific colour and children are instructed to find and stand on a mat of that colour.

Sleeping, Sleeping, All the Children Are Sleeping

Children pretend to sleep when the teacher sings, "Sleeping, sleeping, all the children are sleeping." While children pretend to sleep, the circle leader gives an additional instruction for children to wake up and act out an animal (for example, "You are monkeys!"). Additional rules can be added to make the game more complicated.

Conducting an orchestra

The teacher uses a dowel rod as a conducting baton to lead children in playing musical instruments (for example, jingle bells or maracas). When the conductor waves the baton, children play their instruments. When the conductor puts the baton down, children stop. The conductor then instructs children to play their instruments quickly when the baton moves quickly and slowly when the baton moves slowly. Children are also asked to respond to opposite cues. When the conductor waves the baton, children stop playing their instruments, and when the conductor sets the baton down, children play their instruments.

Drumbeats

Children respond to different drum cues with body movements. Teachers choose actions for children to perform while sitting (for example, clapping or stomping) and while moving around the room (for example, walking or dancing). For example, children are instructed to walk quickly to fast drumming, walk slowly to slow drumming and freeze when the drumming stops. Teachers also ask children to respond to opposite cues (walking slowly to fast drumbeats and quickly to slow drumbeats) and associated different actions with specific drum cues (for example, hopping to fast drumbeats and crawling to slow drumbeats).

Download these resources in A4 format from https://sowattlearning.com

References

Australian Government Department of Education, AGDE. (2022). *Belonging, Being and Becoming: The Early Years Learning Framework for Australia (V2.0)*. Australian Government Department of Education for the Ministerial Council. www.acecqa.gov.au/sites/default/files/2023-01/EYLF-2022-V2.0.pdf

Bautista, A., Williams, K.E., Lee, K., & Ng, S.P. (2024). Early Self-regulation: Kindergarten Teachers' Understandings, Estimates, Indicators, and Intervention Strategies. *Journal of Early Childhood Teacher Education*, 1–22.

Blair, C., Calkins, S., & Gatzke-Kopp, L. (2010). Self-Regulation as the Interface of Emotional and Cognitive Development: Implications for Education and Academic Achievement. *Handbook of Personality and Self-Regulation*, 64–90.

Brackett, M., RULER. https://marcbrackett.com/ruler

Chouinard, M.M. (2007). Children's Questions: A Mechanism for Cognitive Development. *Monographs of the Society for Research in Child Development*, *72*(1), vii–126. https://doi.org/10.1111/j.1540-5834.2007.00412.x

de Wilde, A., Koot, H.M., & van Lier, P.A. (2016). Developmental Links Between Children's Working Memory and their Social Relations with Teachers and Peers in the Early School Years. *Journal of Abnormal Child Psychology*, *44*(1), 19–30.

Diamond, A. (2014). Executive Functions. *Annual Review of Psychology, 64*, 135–168.

Diamond, A. (2016). Why Improving and Assessing Executive Functions Early in Life is Critical. The American Psychological Association.

Diamond, A., & Lee, K. (2011). Interventions Shown to Aid Executive Function Development in Children 4–12 Years Old. *Science, 333*(6045), 959–964.

Diamond, A., & Ling, D.S. (2016). Conclusions About Interventions, Programs, and Approaches for Improving Executive Functions that Appear Justified and Those That, Despite Much Hype, Do Not. *Developmental Cognitive Neuroscience, 18*, 34–48.

Doebel, S. (2020). Rethinking Executive Function and its Development. *Perspectives on Psychological Science, 15*(4), 942–956.

Gathercole, S., & Packiam Alloway, T. (2008). *Working Memory and Learning: A Practical Guide for Teachers*. SAGE Publications.

Gerholm, T., Kallioinen, P., Tonér, S., Frankenberg, S., Kjällander, S., Palmer, A., & Lenz-Taguchi, H. (2019). A Randomized Controlled Trial to Examine the Effect of Two Teaching Methods on Preschool Children's Language and Communication, Executive Functions, Socioemotional Comprehension, and Early Math Skills. *BMC Psychology, 7*, 1–28.

Harms, M.B., & Garrett-Ruffin, S.D. (2023). Disrupting Links Between Poverty, Chronic Stress, and Educational Inequality. *Science of Learning, 8*(1), 50.

Hattie, J., & Timperley, H. (2007). The Power of Feedback. *Review of Educational Research, 77*(1), 81–112.

Howard, S.J., Vasseleu, E., Batterham, M., & Neilsen-Hewett, C. (2020). Everyday Practices and Activities to Improve Pre-school Self-Regulation: Cluster RCT Evaluation of the PRSIST Program. *Frontiers in Psychology, 11*, 137.

Howard, S.J., Vasseleu, E., Neilsen-Hewett, C., de Rosnay, M., Chan, A.Y.C., Johnstone, S., Mavilidi, M., Paas, F., & Melhuish, E.C. (2021). Executive Function and Self-Regulation: Bi-Directional Longitudinal Associations and Prediction of Early Academic Skills. *Frontiers in Psychology, 12*, 733328.

Jacob, R.T., & Parkinson, J. (2015). The Potential for School-Based Interventions that Target Executive Function to Improve Academic Achievement: A Review. *Review of Educational Research, 85*(4), 512–552.

Konovalov, A., & Krajbich, I. (2018). Neurocomputational Dynamics of Sequence Learning. *Neuron, 98*(6), 1282–1293.

Lervåg, A., Hulme, C., & Melby-Lervåg, M. (2018). Unpicking the Developmental Relationship Between Oral Language Skills and Reading Comprehension: It's Simple, but Complex. *Child Development, 89*(5), 1821–1838.

McClelland, M.M., Geldhof, J., Morrison, F., Gestsdóttir, S., Cameron, C., Bowers, E., Duckworth, A., Little, T., & Grammer, J. (2018). Self-regulation. *Handbook of Life Course Health Development*, 275–298.

McClelland, M.M., Ponitz, C.C., Messersmith, E.E., & Tominey, S. (2010). Self-regulation: Integration of Cognition and Emotion. In W. F. Overton & R. M. Lerner (Eds.), *The Handbook of Life-span Development, Vol. 1. Cognition, Ciology, and Methods,* 509–553

McClelland, M.M., Tominey, S.L., Schmitt, S.A., Hatfield, B.E., Purpura, D.J., Gonzales, C.R., & Tracy, A.N. (2019). Red Light, Purple Light! Results of an Intervention to Promote School Readiness for Children from Low-Income Backgrounds. *Frontiers in Psychology, 10*, 2365.

Miyake, A., Friedman, N.P., Emerson, M.J., Witzki, A.H., Howerter, A., & Wager, T.D. (2000). The Unity and Diversity of Executive Functions and their Contributions to Complex 'Frontal Lobe' Tasks: A Latent Variable Analysis. *Cognitive Psychology, 41*(1), 49–100.

Moffitt, T.E., Arseneault, L., Belsky, D., Dickson, N., Hancox, R.J., Harrington, H., Houts, R., Poulton, R., Roberts, B.W., Ross, S., Sears, M.R., Thomson, W.M., & Caspi, A. (2011). A Gradient of Childhood Self-control Predicts Health, Wealth, and Public Safety. *Proceedings of the National Academy of Sciences, 108*(7), 2693–2698.

Morrison, F.J., & Grammer, J.K. (2016). Conceptual Clutter and Measurement Mayhem: Proposals for Cross-disciplinary Integration in Conceptualizing and Measuring Executive Function. In J. A. Griffin, P. McCardle, & L. S. Freund (Eds.), *Executive Function in Preschool-age Children: Integrating Measurement, Neurodevelopment, and Translational Research,* 327–348.

Muir, R.A., Howard, S.J., & Kervin, L. (2023). Interventions and Approaches Targeting Early Self-Regulation or Executive Functioning in Preschools: A Systematic Review. *Educational Psychology Review, 35*(1), 27.

National Scientific Council on the Developing Child. (2010). *Early Experiences Can Alter Gene Expression and Affect Long-Term Development: Working Paper No. 10.* www.developingchild.net

Organisation for Economic Co-operation and Development, OECD. (2012). *Quality in Education*: Supporting Disadvantaged Students and Schools, 3.

Organisation for Economic Co-operation and Development, OECD. (2019). Future of Education and Skills 2030.

Organisation for Economic Co-operation and Development, OECD. (2023). *Education at a Glance 2023: OECD Indicators.* https://doi.org/10.1787/e13bef63-en

Posner, M.I., & Rothbart, M.K. (2007). Research on Attention Networks as a Model for the Integration of Psychological Science. *Annual Review of Psychology, 58*(1), 1–23.

Raver, C.C., & Blair, C. (2020). Developmental Science Aimed at Reducing Inequality: Maximizing the Social Impact of Research on Executive Function in Context. *Infant and Child Development, 29*(1).

Raver, C.C., Jones, S.M., Li-Grining, C., Zhai, F., Bub, K., & Pressler, E. (2011). CSRP's Impact on Low-income Preschoolers' Preacademic Skills: Self-regulation as a Mediating Mechanism. *Child Development, 82*(1), 362–378.

Resnick, M. (2017). *Lifelong Kindergarten: Cultivating Creativity through Projects, Passion, Peers, and Play.* The MIT Press.

Seligman, M. (2004). *The New Era of Positive Psychology.* TED Talk. www.ted.com/talks/martin_seligman_on_the_state_of_psychology

Trentacosta, C.J., & Shaw, D.S. (2009). Emotional Self-Regulation, Peer Rejection, and Antisocial Behavior: Developmental Associations from Early Childhood to Early Adolescence. *Journal of Applied Developmental Psychology, 30*(3), 356–365.

Acknowledgements

I am deeply grateful to the many individuals who have played pivotal roles in the creation of this book.

To my family – my husband, Ken, and daughters, Lorna and Katherine. You are my biggest supporters. I know it can be a pain being around a 'lifelong learner', but I am so grateful for your continued belief in my ability and need to tick off yet another goal. For the numerous times I asked you to proofread drafts, help me format a spreadsheet or simply relied on you for a nourishing feed – thank you!

To Russell Kaplan, my former colleague and friend, thank you for years of collaboration and brainstorming on how to enhance student thinking. Without these discussions and your enthusiasm, SOWATT would have been confined to my head – I was the lucky one who was able to give up my job to pursue the research.

I am really appreciative of Alicia Cohen and the team at Amba Press for supporting my vision for this book for educators and for Rica Dearman's attention to detail in the editing phase. Special thanks also to Debbie Roper and Laura Pearce for your proofreading and invaluable feedback, despite there being a thousand other things you could have been doing instead.

Thank you to the many amazing educators I have met throughout my long career, who have generously shared their craft and inspired me to be the best I can be. There are too many to mention by name, but it would be remiss of me not to mention the wonderful preschool educators at The King David School and Glen Education in Melbourne, who welcomed me into their classrooms to work alongside them to develop SOWATT.

To my PhD supervisors, Professor Steven Howard and Professor Lisa Kervin (AM), who supported me throughout the long and, at times, very challenging research period. Your quiet patience, ability to articulate complex matters so clearly, and your acceptance of me as a colleague was humbling – thank you.

Finally, to Harley, who demanded I step away from my desk at four o'clock each day to go for a walk and some fresh air – even dogs like routines!

Thank you all for your contributions and support.

About the author

Rosalyn Muir has worked in education for more years than she cares to remember and has enjoyed an exciting career around the globe: England, Canada, Sri Lanka, Malaysia, Ireland, Peru, Spain and currently Australia. Her experience across a variety of roles, from classroom teacher and head teacher to advisor and researcher, has reinforced her belief that it is the educators in the classroom who make the greatest difference to the individual child or student.

Her master's degree focused on the professional learning of teachers, and this has also featured in her PhD studies as she researched how best to improve the development of executive functioning and self-regulation in the classroom. Rosalyn is now on a mission to support all educators to reflect on their professional practices to see how they may embed the intentional development of these two constructs into their daily practice.

She believes we need to teach children how to become better learners, and for teachers to learn how to be more effective if we are truly going to improve educational outcomes. Her recent work in early years education sees her as an advocate for building firm foundations on which to build flourishing futures.

Away from education she loves entertaining family and friends around the dinner table, where the emphasis is very much on socialising, rather than cooking, which she leaves to her husband. Rosalyn is an avid park runner, who will be found each Saturday morning either running or volunteering at an event somewhere in the world. She has even been known to plan holidays around this hobby/obsession!

The family dog, Harley, an energetic Hungarian Vizsla, ensures she gets daily exercise and may also be an indication that she has finally put down roots in Melbourne, Australia.

www.ingramcontent.com/pod-product-compliance
Lightning Source LLC
Chambersburg PA
CBHW050247120526
44590CB00016B/2252